Constructive Journalism

This book offers a deep and comprehensive overview of constructive journalism, setting out the guiding principles and practices for a journalism that aims to do more than simply inform about problems.

In this authoritative yet concise volume, Peter Bro asks what does constructive journalism mean, what are the underlying principles, how is it practiced, and in what ways does it differ from other types of journalism? Drawing on studies of the rapidly growing number of works by both journalism practitioners and researchers, the book reaches beyond these questions to show how the notion of being constructive has been a part of journalism from the very beginning of the profession.

This introduction to what constructive journalism is and was and what it can accomplish will guide new journalists; journalism, media, and mass communication students; and scholars working on journalistic theory and practice.

Peter Bro is Professor, PhD, and Director of the Centre for Journalism at the University of Southern Denmark.

Routledge Focus on Journalism Studies

When Media Succumbs to Rising Authoritarianism
Cautionary Tales from Venezuela's Recent History
Edited by Ezequiel Korin and Paromita Pain

Front-Page Scotland
Newspapers and the Scottish Independence Referendum
David Patrick

Public Television in Poland
Political Pressure and Public Service Media in a Post-communist Country
Agnieszka Węglińska

Election Politics and the Mass Press in Long Edwardian Britain
Christopher Shoop-Worrall

Journalism's Racial Reckoning
The News Media's Pivot to Diversity and Inclusion
Brad Clark

Re-examining the UK Newspaper Industry
Marc Edge

Humanitarian Journalists
Covering Crises from a Boundary Zone
Martin Scott, Kate Wright, and Mel Bunce

Constructive Journalism
Precedents, Principles, and Practices
Peter Bro

Constructive Journalism
Precedents, Principles, and Practices

Peter Bro

LONDON AND NEW YORK

First published 2024
by Routledge
4 Park Square, Milton Park, Abingdon, Oxon OX14 4RN

and by Routledge
605 Third Avenue, New York, NY 10158

Routledge is an imprint of the Taylor & Francis Group, an informa business

© 2024 Peter Bro

The right of Peter Bro to be identified as author of this work has been asserted in accordance with sections 77 and 78 of the Copyright, Designs and Patents Act 1988.

All rights reserved. No part of this book may be reprinted or reproduced or utilised in any form or by any electronic, mechanical, or other means, now known or hereafter invented, including photocopying and recording, or in any information storage or retrieval system, without permission in writing from the publishers.

Trademark notice: Product or corporate names may be trademarks or registered trademarks, and are used only for identification and explanation without intent to infringe.

British Library Cataloguing-in-Publication Data
A catalogue record for this book is available from the British Library

ISBN: 978-1-032-51609-7 (hbk)
ISBN: 978-1-032-51611-0 (pbk)
ISBN: 978-1-003-40309-8 (ebk)

DOI: 10.4324/9781003403098

Typeset in Times New Roman
by codeMantra

Contents

	List of figures	*vii*
	Foreword	*ix*
	Acknowledgments	*xi*
1	Introduction to constructive journalism	1
2	Precedents of constructive journalism	17
3	Principles of constructive journalism	41
4	Practices of constructive journalism	62
5	Conclusion	81
	Index	*93*

Figures

1.1	The journalistic compass	8
2.1	Concepts and catchphrases used to describe active types of journalism	34
3.1	The active journalism continuum	52
4.1	Four approaches to the selection and presentation of problems and potentials	66
4.2	Constructive journalism's consensual, controversial, and deviant issues	70
4.3	Sourcing practices in constructive journalism	73
5.1	The journalistic compass	84

Foreword

"The Devil's mirror" is a familiar – and frightening – reference for millions of people around the world. The mirror appears in one of Hans Christian Andersen's fairytales, *The Snow Queen* (1961/1845), where the Devil has constructed a mirror that distorts whatever it reflects: All the good things in life disappear, while all the bad things in life are enlarged. In the first part of the story, the mirror breaks into billions of pieces, and the fragments find their way into people's eyes, so they can only see what Andersen describes as "the bad side of things." *The Snow Queen* is truly one of the darker fairy tales by the world-known Danish storyteller, and growing up, I often thought with horror of the Devil's mirror. The story has stayed with me, not only because I am a Dane, working in the city of Odense where Hans Christian Andersen grew up and where people from all over the world come to visit his place of birth. The story also stayed with me when I started studying journalism and in time became responsible for educating present and future practitioners, for, in many ways, the Devil's mirror epitomizes how journalists work.

Generations of journalists have made a professional point out of presenting problems, big or small, and more or less pressing, while largely overlooking what goes well in the world. As it will become clear in this book, there are many reasons for this. None of these reasons, however, has to do with the fact that contemporary journalists could be counted among those unfortunates in Hans Christians Andersen's story who are left emotionally cold forever, because fragments from the Devil's mirror have found their way to the hearts of people and caused their hearts to become "a lump of ice" (Andersen, 1961/1845, 260). On the contrary, most if not all of the journalists, editors, and owners of news organizations I have encountered in classrooms, newsrooms, and boardrooms believe their work can truly help the world become a better place. Indeed, as the book will show, the canons and creeds in journalism, more generally, and the ethical standards and statements from prominent news organizations and newspersons, more specifically, also call on journalists to take a social responsibility.

Recently, however, it has become clear that there are many other ways of doing that than simply pointing out problems and leaving it to other people to decide what to do – if anything – about the problems. Under names such as "constructive journalism" – and associated concepts such as "solutions journalism" and "problem-solving journalism" – scores of journalists, editors, and owners of news organizations from all over the world have started experimenting with new ways of aiding, assisting, and servicing the public in making the world a better place. This book describes the founding principles and practices of what constructive journalism is and discusses how these particular norms and forms of journalism relate to key concepts of journalism, such as impartiality, objectivity, and social responsibility. The book also discusses differences and similarities between various ways of working constructively and delineates the historical precedents of constructive journalism. The latter is equally important. For when studying the history of journalism, it becomes clear that journalism that aims to do more than simply present problems has a long history and has been promoted, prompted, and supported by some of the craft's most iconic figures.

So far, this long history of constructive journalism has largely been left untold by both practitioners and researchers, and this lack of historical understanding is perhaps not surprising. Focusing on what is new(s) is after all the driving force for many of us who engage with journalism. But when we forget, are unaware of, or simply ignore the traditions of journalism, we tend to repeat the same discussions about the proper roles and responsibilities of journalism, and our ahistorical approach has long stood in the way of learning from past examples and experiences, and developing journalism. So, while this book focuses very much on where journalism is right now and where it is heading, it is also a book about the origins of journalism. The following chapters are written in the belief – based on my own experiences as researcher, lecturer, and board member of media companies – that "nothing is as practical as a good theory." This is particularly the case when theoretical insights can be turned into models, visual and verbal, that practitioners and researchers alike can use to sharpen their thinking and strengthen their technical skills, and as I hope to show throughout this book, journalists are not the only ones who can be constructive when they put their mind to it.

Peter Bro
Odense, March 2023

Reference

Andersen, Hans Christian (1961/1844) "Snedronningen" [*The Snow Queen*]. In *Samlede Eventyr og Historier* [Collected Adventures and Stories], edited by H. C. Andersen, 259–285. København. Hans Reitzels Forlag.

Acknowledgments

Alcohol and academic work might seem like incompatible entities, but this book would never have been written were it not for the Carlsberg Foundation, the parent company of the Carlsberg Brewery. The Foundation is one of the biggest supporters of scholarly work in Denmark, and the appointment as a Carlsberg Foundation Fellow for 2022 made it possible for me to take a year off to write this book. During that year, I have often thought with gratitude of this opportunity to focus on what I personally consider one of the most important and pertinent issues within journalism studies these years: constructive journalism. This gratefulness has been especially pronounced whenever I found myself at birthdays, receptions, picnics, and other social gatherings where products from Carlsberg were available.

When it comes to the scholarly outcome of this one-year writer's leave, my main thanks go to those journalistic practitioners and researchers who have kindly shared their thoughts. Some of them might not even know how their work – in written, audible, or visual formats – has inspired the work in this book. But I am certain that many of the people I have met as part of this research project will recognize their own important contribution on the following pages. Indeed many of them are credited throughout the book and in the reference list. A few people, however, deserve special mention for sharing their thoughts in writing and taking time to meet with me whenever questions arise.

So, thank you Cathrine Gyldensted and Ulrik Haagerup for readily answering all my questions and for taking the time to explain your own work and journalistic visions. Thank you also to colleagues – from both sides of the Atlantic – who took part in the inspiring conference organized by the Centre for Journalism at University of Southern Denmark and Constructive Institute at Aarhus University in Denmark in October 2022. A special thank you, also, to my co-organizers of the conference about the state of research on constructive journalism: Morten Skovsgaard, University of Southern Denmark, and Peter Damgaard, Aarhus University. Our discussions about the state of constructive journalism before and after the conference were just as important to me as the conference itself.

Finally, it is worth remembering that journalists, editors, and others working for the news media at times include statements about their relation to the issues they cover and the news sources they rely on in their work. This is a sound principle, so for the sake of transparency it is worth mentioning here that I, for years, have been "a sympathetic, although critical" observer, as I have previously described my engagement with the constructive journalism movement (Bro, 2019). I have, for example, participated in conferences hosted by the Constructive Institute and produced book chapters with each of the two founders of the movement (Bro, 2012; Bro & Gyldensted, 2021), and I am currently also a member of the advisory board at Constructive Institute. While I do not myself think that these types of collaborations and commitments, both the past and the present, interfere negatively with my scholarly involvement in this issue, it should certainly be known to readers of this book who can then make their own judgments about the importance of this involvement.

References

Bro, Peter (2019) "Constructive journalism: Principles, precedents, and practices." *Journalism* 20 (4): 504–519.

Bro, Peter (2012) "Historien om den nyttige nyhedsformidling" ["The history of usefull news reporting"]. In *En konstruktiv nyhed* [A Constructive News Story], edited by Ulrik Haagerup, 129–143. Århus: Ajour.

Bro, Peter & Cathrine Gyldensted (2021) "Constructive journalism: Portraying the world accurately through positive psychology." In *Reporting Beyond the Problem: From Civic Journalism to Solutions Journalism*, edited by Karen McIntyre and Nicole Dahmen, 29–46. New York: Peter Lang.

1 Introduction to constructive journalism

What is news? Journalism researchers have offered many different answers to that question over the years, and the question continues to be one of the primary objects of study in scholarly circles. But for journalistic practitioners for whom the answer to that question has immediate practical implications, there are some working definitions that have stood the test of time. One of the most popular definitions, also known by many people outside the news industry, states that "news is what somebody somewhere wants to suppress; all the rest is advertising." Who originally coined the definition is still disputed, but journalistic icons like Joseph Pulitzer, William Randolph Hearst, and not least Lord Northcliffe, who owned scores of English newspapers at the turn of the last century, are some of the person's most often credited. Lord Northcliffe, the British media magnate, Alfred Harmsworth, who was ennobled in 1904, is one of the obvious candidates. Northcliffe was known for conjuring catchphrases that distilled his understanding of what news was, so it was effectively instilled in his many journalists and editors.

Lord Northcliffe was not alone. At the turn of the last century, when journalism developed into a full-time profession rather than something book printers, politicians, and professors did on the side, editors and owners of newspapers often pinned their views on what news was on plaques hung on the walls in their newsrooms.[1] That way, their journalists were reminded daily of what news was, and although the wording varied, the working definitions were often based on the same core set of values: News should contain something that was problematic for "somebody somewhere." Misuse of public funds, corruption, crime, accidents, injuries, and a host of other problems were considered good news, and reporters were strategically dispersed, so they collectively could discover what happened at fire and police stations, hospitals, political institutions, and other places where problems were known to surface. "If it bleeds, it leads" read another widely used instruction to news reporters, and this approach has continued to this day, where journalists are increasingly trained in classrooms at universities and journalism schools rather than in the newsrooms.

DOI: 10.4324/9781003403098-1

Publishing what is problematic to somebody somewhere is an approach that makes sense on the surface of things, particularly around the turn of the last century. Before that, most newspapers were essentially views-papers that promoted the interests of others, including but not limited to royalty, nobility, political parties, religious groups, and commercial enterprises. They were considered "organs of opinion" as it has been rightly described (Chalaby, 2000, 36). Starting in the late nineteenth century, however, owners, editors, and journalists around the world strove to separate news from views, to make newspapers a business in their own right, and to distance their media products from the interests of previous owners and sponsors. This new distance was marked by both the form and the focus of news. If views were included in this new era, they increasingly appeared in the form of the newly invented *inter-views* (Schudson, 1995).[2] As a result, views put forward by persons and organizations outside the newsroom were gradually separated graphically from the text produced by journalists by the use of bold, italics, pullout quotes, quotation marks, and other textual markers. Or they were moved to special sections like the editorial pages or the op-eds (short for "opposite editorial pages"), where views could also be separated from news by way of the layout of pages (Barnhurst & Nerone, 2001).

People like Northcliffe, Pulitzer, and Hearst, who owned, ordered, and organized the work at these new types of news-papers – a name now better befitted – went further than that. They also changed the focus of news and started to put a premium on problems – big or small, more or less pressing – since they believed this new focus would distinguish them further from the views-papers of the past, which often contained positive reports about the ideas, issues, and institutions their owners supported. This new generation of newspaper owners believed that a focus on problems could help galvanize their more neutral and impartial newspapers against criticism. In hindsight, none of these efforts to change the form and focus is surprising. Being neutral and impartial became a business imperative, since it ensured that newspapers could cater to larger, diverse, and more dispersed audiences rather than pander to smaller segments of the public, and Northcliffe, Pulitzer, and Hearst amassed fortunes that made them some of the world's wealthiest men. Presenting problems therefore became a fixture – at times even fixed on the walls in newsrooms in the form of catchphrases or instructive concepts – for the first generation of journalists, and it has remained so for many later generations.

One of the most consistent research results from the profession of journalism researchers that have developed alongside the practice of journalism is the continued interest in presenting problems. Realizing this continued preference for problems does not require a PhD degree, tenure at a university, or the skillset of a professional journalism researcher. Have a look in the latest newspaper, listen to or watch one of the latest news programs, and consult one of the digital platforms where more and more people receive their news, and you will probably find that many, if not most – or even all – elements at any given time focus on problems. Some problems may be new in comparison with the problems that news workers around the turn of the last century were sent out to find. Attacks on military installations by hackers, collisions between self-driving cars, the shortcomings of cryptocurrencies, and many other problems were not known more than a hundred years ago. But while the nature of problems may have changed as our societies develop, the culture of news reporting has been remarkably consistent in form and focus.

As a result, much of what is presented as news today continues to be a problem for "somebody somewhere" in the world. At least, this is how things have been for centuries. For recently things has started to change in more and more newsrooms around the world.

Changing perspectives from problems to solutions

Journalism researchers have not monopolized the criticism of the news media's premium on problems, and in a newspaper column in 2008 entitled "Constructive news," the news director of the Danish Broadcasting Company, Ulrik Haagerup, reflected on what he considered the main problem of the news media, including the news division he was responsible for running:

> A good news story is a bad story, and Danish news media have for years flowed over with them: terror threats, shooting incidents, bankruptcy, downturns, threatening diseases, dramatic accidents, suicide bombs, hurricanes, hunger, death, destruction and politicians who cannot agree. And then there is the weather: The gray weather continues.
> (Haagerup, 2008)

In this column, Haagerup called on his own and other news organizations to consider working more "constructively" and more specifically focus on what goes well in society. The column was the first time a wider audience was introduced to the concept of "constructive news," and both the diagnosis of the ills of journalism and the suggested cure soon gave rise to discussions in the Danish news media, national conferences, and books about what was by then also referred to as "constructive journalism." The first book-length presentation of constructive journalism was an anthology in Danish, entitled *A Constructive News Story* edited by Haagerup (2012a).[3] In this book, politicians, news editors, journalists, scholars, and other Danes described and discussed why traditional journalism needed to change and what the concept of constructive journalism could entail for journalism, the news media, and society.

Many points and perspectives from this anthology were later expanded into a monograph, *Constructive News* (Haagerup, 2014), written for an international audience. By then, Haagerup was joined by Cathrine Gyldensted in

4 *Introduction to constructive journalism*

advocating, at home and abroad, for constructive journalism. Gyldensted, who contributed to the anthology from 2012 with "The ghost from Watergate," was originally trained as a journalist and had worked as an investigative reporter for the Danish Broadcasting Company before studying positive psychology as a graduate student. Gyldensted's graduate work, not least her master's thesis from the University of Pennsylvania, entitled "Innovating News Journalism through Positive Psychology" (2011), became the basis for several publications, including a handbook in Danish about constructive journalism (Gyldensted & Bjerre, 2014) and the monograph *From Mirrors to Movers* (2015), in which she encouraged journalists to focus more on "positive," "inspirational," and "solution-based news."

The monographs, anthologies, op-eds, and other publications helped promote the basic idea of constructive journalism, and still more journalists, editors, and owners of news organizations around the world began to experiment with their own takes on constructive practices. These experiments in turn led to new publications that introduced others to the thoughts and sparked even more interest among practitioners. Even though there has been criticism of constructive journalism from the very beginning the results of the experiments, publications and others types of presentations have been a virtuous cycle that has popularized constructive journalism, and the experiments have been helped and even accelerated by initiatives.[4] In 2017, Constructive Institute was established at Aarhus University in Denmark, founded and directed by Haagerup, and today the institute arranges conferences, workshops, and other events around the world. Constructive Institute also hosts a fellowship program where fellows experiment with new ways of working with constructive journalism, for example, in the coverage of politics, sports, and science.

In time, other universities and journalism schools have introduced their own programs, classes, and courses focusing on constructive journalism, and within 15 years after Haagerup first introduced the concept of "constructive news" to a wider audience, more than a handful of books (see, e.g., Gyldensted, 2015; Gyldensted & Bjerre, 2014; Haagerup, 2012a, 2014, 2017; Holmaas, 2019; Jørgensen & Risbro, 2021; May, 2020; McIntyre & Dahmen, 2021), several PhD dissertations (see, e.g., McIntyre, 2015), close to a hundred journal articles (see, e.g., Ahva & Hautakangas, 2018; Bro, 2019; From & Kristensen, 2018; Hermans & Drok, 2018; Hermans & Prins, 2020); Krüger et al., 2022; Lough & McIntyre, K., 2019; Lough & McIntyre, 2021; McIntyre & Gyldensted, 2017: Thier et al., 2019), and special issues in flagship journals, such as *Journalism* (Mast et al., 2019) and *Journalism Practice* (Ahva & Hautakangas, 2018), had been published with specific reference to constructive journalism, all of which has accelerated the spread of the concept and made its premises, principles, and practices known among journalistic practitioners and researchers around the world.

Other things have also helped popularize the notion that journalists should do more than present problems. Almost simultaneously with the rise and spread of the concept of constructive journalism, other practitioners and researchers – most notably in the US and UK – have worked with "solutions journalism." While the concept had been used before (Benesch, 1998) – as part of the so-called "public journalism movement" – things really took off when the Solutions Journalism Network was established in 2013, and among its founders are David Bornstein and Tina Rosenberg, who developed the weekly column "Fixes" in *The New York Times*. According to the network, it has worked with more than 500 news organizations and 20,000 journalists worldwide to develop news stories that focus more on solutions to problems rather than just problems.[5] As is the case with constructive journalism, several news outlets have introduced regular segments, columns, and news story formats with a specific focus on "solutions" on a monthly, weekly, or even daily basis.

Before then, journalists in other countries – not least France – worked to bring about a similar change in journalism. In 2004, a group of French journalists and editors formed Reporters d'Espoirs (Reporters of Hope) and started giving out the so-called solution prizes in collaboration with the UN. Within a few years, this group has grown into an association that boasts an impressive number of conferences and workshops for news organizations and persons around the world, and today the organization writes on its website that it has "worked on 'solutions journalism', 'impact journalism' and 'constructive journalism' over the past 15 years."[6] "Journalism that makes you act" is one of the descriptions used by Reporters d'Espoirs. Both these movements are either directly associated or comparable with the constructive journalism movement, and even though they differ in important ways, more things unite them than divide them. What they share is both the diagnosis and cure for journalism and – crucially – the foundational belief that journalism should do more than simply present problems in order to service the public.

Four ways to service the public

"Insofar as journalism is grounded, it is grounded in the public," James Carey famously noted (1987, 5), and as views-papers gave way to regular newspapers, the concept of the public has become a cornerstone of modern journalism. Few if any journalistic representatives have stressed this point more categorically than one of modern journalism's first and strongest supporters, Joseph Pulitzer. Throughout his lifetime, Pulitzer bought several viewspapers that promoted the interests of political parties and turned them into, in essence, more neutral newspapers. Servicing the public is "the supreme end" for journalism, he wrote at the height of his success (1904, 46), and in a seminal essay about the importance of journalism, Pulitzer pledged to support the development of a public-spirited press and also presented his elaborate plans to help ensure such an endeavor. He vowed to use part of his fortune to fund what today is known as the Pulitzer Prizes, one of which is awarded for the best example of "public service." This was meant to inspire current practitioners.

Pulitzer also wanted to infuse future practitioners with a public service orientation and he therefore endowed Columbia University with sufficient funds to set up what was supposed to be the first journalism schools in the US. Contractual difficulties and lengthy discussions between the university and Pulitzer prolonged the process (Farrar, 1998), so the first journalism school was established in 1908 at the University of Missouri, Kansas, at the initiative of Walter Williams. Williams, who had also owned a newspaper, however, harbored the same sentiments as Pulitzer and inspired many generations of journalists with that very understanding of whom and what a journalists should work for. He did this through the journalism school, one of the first textbooks about journalism that he co-wrote with a colleague at the journalism school in Kansas and, not least, through his famous *The Journalist's Creed* (1914). The creed has reportedly been translated to more than 100 languages, reprinted numerous times; adorns the walls at the National Press Club in Washington DC (Farrar, 1998); and still appears in courses, classes, and curriculums at many journalism schools around the world.[7]

The creed starts as follows:

> I believe that the public journal is a public trust; that all connected with it are, to the full measure of their responsibility, trustees for the public; that acceptance of a lesser service than the public service is betrayal of this trust.

To this very day, journalistic practitioners in many, if not most, parts of the world use the concept of the public as what Carey described as the "good term of journalism – the be-all and end-all, the term without which the entire enterprise fails to make sense" (1987, 5). While practitioners might not always think of the implications of what to some might seem like an abstract and archaic concept like "the public," they rely on this notion of the public in their own work and in the support from other persons and organizations outside the newsrooms.

"The public has a right to know" has become a common catchphrase among journalists, editors, and owners of news organizations when they encounter reluctant news sources, or when journalists face accusations of malpractice or wrongdoing. "The public" is deployed as a rhetorical device – or, to put it more bluntly, a linguistic ploy – whether journalists are on the defensive or the offensive. The concept is also used by others, outside newsrooms, to justify the work of journalists and their employers. In many countries, especially in the Western world, journalists are offered rights that do not befall others because of their status as representatives of the public. These rights include crossing police barricades or following demonstrators into places (public buildings, private homes, etc.) where they might not normally be allowed. In some countries, news organizations receive economic subsidies and other types of support as representatives of the public, and while some countries have state-financed public service media, even private media can be offered financial, legal, or other types of support with reference to the "public service" they provide (Skovsgaard & Bro, 2017)

Occasionally, critics accuse journalists and their news organizations for working for others, such as "advertisers," "sources," "owners," and "editors". But ideally, journalists' obligation is to the public, and "[f]or all that has changed about journalism, its purpose has remained remarkably constant," Tom Rosenstiel and Bill Kovach conclude in *The Elements of Journalism* (2014, 16). However, despite the widespread agreement about *whom* journalists principally should work for, it has been less clear *how* journalists in their daily practice should provide this service. Here, the popularization of constructive journalism, solutions journalism, and associated forms of journalism highlights that there are several ways to service the public. According to the so-called "journalistic compass" (Bro, 2018), there are at least four such major approaches. Some of the most ardent chroniclers of the constructive turn in journalism kindly refer to the compass as a helpful theoretical framework when it comes to describing similarities and differences between more traditional forms of journalism and the new movements (McIntyre & Lough, 2021).[8]

In essence, the compass incorporates four corners of the world of journalism and helps its users navigate in two directions or dimensions: passive–active (east–west) and deliberative–representative (north–south). On the horizontal axis, a passive journalist is content with mirroring what happens in the world; an active journalist attempts to help the public solve its problems. The vertical axis relates to persons, professions, and organizations who are included in the news. In much journalism, news sources are persons who represent parts of the public in their capacity as, for example, leaders of a political party, members of parliament, and persons who direct or oversee unions, companies, organizations, etc. In other cases, private citizens are included, and all members of the public are invited to take part in the public deliberations in the news media.

The horizontal axis in the compass relates to the *purpose of journalism*; the vertical axis relates to the *perspective of journalism*, and when the two axes are combined (see Figure 1.1), they collectively form four fields. Each field describes a particular set of responsibilities, essentially different roles, for journalists in terms of their purpose and perspective (passive-representative, passive-deliberative, active-representative, and active-deliberative). For the sake of clarity, each role has been described metaphorically as different breeds of dogs. The watchdog focuses on persons and organizations that represent the

8 Introduction to constructive journalism

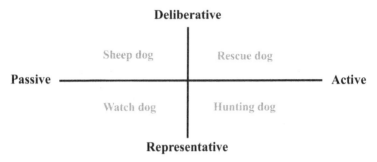

Figure 1.1 The journalistic compass.

public and is passive to the extent that it simply reports the actions, attitudes, etc., of public representatives. The hunting dog is more aggressive than the watchdog and actively works to help solve societal problems by enlisting the help of the public representative. The rescue dog is also active, but journalists who navigate toward the upper-right corner in the compass will attempt to motivate private citizens to act.

As such, the watchdog and the hunting dog have the same perspective but different purposes; the hunting dog and the rescue dog have a common purpose but different perspectives. Finally, the sheepdog is passive like the watchdog (both are situated on the passive side) but has a focus on citizens like the rescue dog (both are placed in the upper half). But while including citizens is a means to an end for the rescue dog, who is working to prompt action among other things to help solve societal problems, the sheepdog works to include all members of society – private citizens as well as decision-makers – in public deliberations in the news media. Overall, the compass illustrates four ideal-typical ways in which journalists individually and collectively can service the public. The four roles are ideal-typical, in the sense that in this pure form, they do not always correspond perfectly with all current practices in journalism. This is, of course, the case for all models. Models are not meant to illustrate all complexities in the world but rather to carve out the most important constitutive elements of the phenomena they model, and here the compass includes several distinguishing characteristics that are particularly helpful in describing and discussing similarities and differences between traditional and more recent types of journalism.

The journalistic compass has a dual capacity as all symbolic representations.[9] First, journalists can use the compass – as "symbol for" (Carey, 1992/1975) – to navigate the world of news, and generations of journalists have been taught to use the compass in just this way. Whenever journalists – both future practitioners at journalism schools and contemporary practitioners in newsrooms – are charged with finding new news stories, the compass can help them navigate. Should they, for example, attempt to include stories and sources from the public or rather focus on representatives of the public, and how should they approach their news stories? Should they simply present the news and leave it to others to decide what to do, or should they be more active and attempt to help society solve its problems? The answers to these questions and the appropriate navigation can differ from story to story, but the compass shows that there are several ways to do news work. In this capacity as a "symbol for," the compass can help current and future journalists decide where to find a new(s) story and how to present it to their audience.

The news compass can also be used as a "symbol of," and while journalists and editors can use the compass to guide their work, researchers and others can use the compass as an analytical tool, for example, as a framework for analyzing news stories – or an entire newspaper – to determine what journalistic roles and responsibilities are most prevailing. It can be used to analyze the past and present and to probe the future. Previous market research suggests that that news audiences generally value the watchdog most and find that they get too little deliberative journalism in comparison with the representative focus, but what is perhaps most noteworthy is that surveys suggest that audiences prefer the entire dog kennel, metaphorically speaking. In other words, they value all four roles. This corresponds with Michael Schudson's suggestion that the "news media should be self-consciously schizophrenic in their efforts to perform a democratic political function" (1995, 211–212), insofar as journalists, editors, and owners of news organizations should perform several societal roles simultaneously and let these roles supplement one another.

The principles, precedents, and practices of constructive journalism

All four ideal types of journalism in the compass can rightfully be said to service the public, but for now, it is important to note that when the journalistic compass is used as an analytical framework to compare more traditional journalism with constructive journalism (and associated movements), the latter are situated in the right-hand side of the compass. For the early proponents and promoters and the many later supporters of constructive journalism, it is not enough for journalism to simply "mirror" – to quote Cathrine Gyldensted – what is problematic in the world. Constructive journalists are "more active," in the words of Haagerup (2012b, 218), insofar as they believe they have a responsibility to focus on more than problems. There is, however, little agreement among supporters of constructive journalism about what "more active" entails and just how active journalists could – and should – take responsibility for.

Some journalists, editors, and owners of news organizations believe it is sufficient to present solutions to be constructive, while others believe journalism should motivate or even activate the public or its representatives to solve problems. Still others believe journalists should engage in issues to help bring about change. In short, there are several ways to be active, several sub-roles and different types of responsibility. The same complexity applies to the perspective of constructive journalism. Some constructive journalists orient themselves towards the public; others orient themselves towards politicians, company executives, and other authoritative decision-makers in society. The early proponents of these new, more constructive approaches, Ulrik Haagerup and Cathrine Gyldensted, have not done much to minimize the "conceptual clarity" (Bro, 2019, 506), and as other researchers have noted the definition of the concept is "somewhat vague" (From & Kristensen, 2018, 716).

Both of the early pioneers do offer several definitions of what constructive journalism is – and what it is not – but they also maintain the need to be open to new developments, and their definitions are, in many ways, open for interpretation by journalistic practitioners. One of the preferred definitions at Constructive Institute echoes what Haagerup, founder and director, has stated in writing and visual presentations over the past years:

> Constructive journalism is a response to increasing tabloidization, sensationalism and negativity bias of the news media today. It is an approach that aims to provide audiences with a fair, accurate and contextualized picture of the world, without overemphasizing the negative and what is going wrong.[10]

Gyldensted has also introduced several definitions over the years. The definition quoted below, which she co-wrote with Karen McIntyre (McIntyre was the first to write a doctoral dissertation about constructive journalism), is frequently referenced:

> An emerging form of journalism that involves applying positive psychology techniques to news processes and production in an effort to create productive and engaging coverage, while holding true to journalism's core functions.
>
> (2017, 23)

Both definitions point to an important distinction between a type of journalism that focuses on problems, what Haagerup describes as "the negative" and "what is going wrong," and a journalism that points to what he elsewhere describes as "what goes well" and "could work well" in the future. Gyldensted and McIntyre also direct our attention to the latter when they refer to "positive psychology techniques" that prompt journalists to present stories that can "improve individual and societal well-being" (McIntyre & Gyldensted, 2017, 23). However, the two definitions differ in terms of what constructive journalism is meant to accomplish. Haagerup's definition contains almost as many words about what constructive journalism should counter as about what it is supposed to do: "provide audiences with a fair, accurate and contextualized picture of the world." Gyldensted and McIntyre are more precise, at least in the initial part of their definition: "create productive and engaging coverage" that holds "true to journalism's core functions." Their respective definitions point to different approaches, but neither implication – a "fair, accurate and contextualized picture" and to hold "true to journalism's core functions" – can be considered either controversial or precise as far as what constructive journalism is meant to accomplish.

To be fair, both Haagerup and Gyldensted have written extensively about constructive journalism and pointed to inspirational examples that more thoroughly, thoughtfully, and not least elaborately introduce journalistic practitioners and researchers to different aspects of what constructive journalism is, what it is not, and what it could be in the future. But both have deliberately chosen not to define their approaches narrowly. "Experiment with new ideas, new questions, new angles, and new ways. Find out what works, and what needs to be corrected," Ulrik Haagerup suggested in *Constructive News* (2014, 113), and the Constructive Institute engages in a wide variety of experiments, some with focus on private citizens and some with focus on society's authoritative decision-makers. Cathrine Gyldensted made a similar point in her book *From Mirrors to Movers*, namely that constructive journalism is "not a static domain but will evolve as the research underpinning method and application evolve" (2015, 174). She has maintained this position in later writings and continues to see "an organic domain, that will need to be revised, matured and progressed as we go along" (cf. Bro, 2019).

While proponents, promoters, and supporters largely agree on what is problematic with more traditional forms of journalism, the suggested cure comes with quite a bit of conceptual elasticity. It was there from the beginning and has inspired supporters of the different movements to come up with other concepts to better describe what they believe are the most important features.[11] While this has helped clarify things for some, it has increased confusion elsewhere. Indeed, even some proponents, promoters, and supporters of the new active forms of journalism disagree about how new and old concepts are best understood, and some have introduced entirely new principles and practices. In line with his call to "[e]xperiment with new ideas, new questions, new angles and new ways," Haagerup (2014, 113) sees constructive journalism as more than a focus on solutions. In time, he has come to perceive and present constructive journalism as being based on three pillars: looking for solutions, embracing nuances, and "engaging and facilitating the public in debate."[12] This third pillar corresponds with the deliberative perspective in the journalistic compass, but the three pillars have caused confusion about what is most important in constructive journalism and how the pillars relate to one another.

The conceptual elasticity has left room for myths and misunderstandings among both journalistic practitioners and researchers – supporters and opponents alike (Bro, 2019). While it has had advantages in the short run by attracting the interest of many who are dissatisfied with traditional types of journalism and/or have ideas about how to develop journalism in new directions, it might have disadvantages in the longer run. If we study the development of journalism in the nineteenth, twentieth, and twenty-first century, it becomes clear that constructive journalism – both as a concept and as a set of principles and practices – has little news value. Indeed, what we today describe as constructive journalism was essentially born long before this approached was baptized. Attempts to "move" the world, in Gyldensted's words, has a long history, and such attempts were even promoted and actively prompted by the founding fathers of modern journalism, including Pulitzer, Hearst, and Northcliffe. The history of journalism, however, also shows that every time active movements have developed, the lack of conceptual precision and authoritative accounts has eventually led to their demise.

The fate of these latest attempts to advance constructive journalism and other more active types of journalism might therefore very well rest on our ability as journalistic practitioners and researchers to clarify the similarities and differences between various types of journalism, including the ways in which contemporary journalists, editors, and owners of news organizations work to become more constructive. This book aims to help with this process, and it will hopefully become clearer what constructive journalism – solutions journalism, action journalism, public journalism, civic journalism, and the many other names practitioners and researchers have used to describe similar attempts – and its inherent journalistic principles more concretely entail. It will hopefully also become clearer how these new approaches relate to some of the foundational principles of journalism, including neutrality and responsibility, and how these principles relate to different practices. These aspects will be addressed in the following chapters.

Chapter 2 describes and discusses the precedents of constructive journalism, and it becomes clear that many of the issues that contemporary practitioners are debating – including how passive or active journalists could and should be – have been recurring themes for centuries. However, none of the attempts has become more lasting contributions to the development of journalism, even if these previous attempts have been heralded by some of the craft's most prominent figures. One of the main reasons is the lack of clarity of the basic principles of journalism, especially how active journalists can be without conflicting with other foundational norms that were instituted with the birth of modern journalism. In Chapter 3 about the principles of constructive journalism, it becomes clear that there are several ways in which journalists can be constructive and different degrees to which journalists can actively work to move the world. Chapter 4 describes and discusses the ways in which these principles are operationalized into concrete practices, and it explains what it takes to practice different types of constructive journalism. The book concludes with a discussion of how we – journalistic practitioners and researchers – can ensure that our experiments to strengthen journalism sustain us rather than fail us, and this final chapter (Chapter 5) also introduced

Introduction to constructive journalism 13

a new definition of constructive journalism that can hopefully help us in this endeavor.

Notes

1 Joel Wiener (2011) and Joseph Campbell (2001), among others, have described this way of disciplining reporters by way of posters, plaques, and other platforms for directives placed directly in newsrooms.
2 Michael Schudson tells the fascinating story of the rise and spread of this practice in *Question Authority: A History of the News Interview in American Journalism, 1860s–1930s* (1995/1994).
3 For those with an immense interest in the historical background of the constructive journalism movement, it is worth noting that the column from 2008, where Haagerup introduced the concept of "constructive news," also came to inspire the publication of an anthology a few years later (Haslebo & Haslebo, 2010). Haagerup contributed to the book with a chapter about constructive news that contains several of the same points, examples, and perspectives that he came to address in his own later books.
4 Constructive journalism has been debated from the very beginning. In 2010, the Danish trade magazine, *Journalisten*, that covers journalism and the news media, interviewed a number of Danish editors and news directors about the new movement. "We should not be part of the team that solves problems," the director of news at the competing national broadcasting company proclaimed, while an editor-in-chief for one of the newspapers with the highest circulation noted that "we must not distort reality if it is ugly" (cf. Andreassen, 2010).
5 The numbers appear on the website for *The Solutions Journalism Network* (https://www.solutionsjournalism.org – accessed March 1, 2023).
6 The numbers appear on the website for *Reporters d'Espoirs* (https://reportersdespoirs.org – accessed March 1, 2023).
7 The creed first appeared in 1914 when it was included in the yearly edition of the style manual at the journalism school in Missouri (Farrar, 1998). Later, it was included in a textbook co-written by Walter Williams and a colleague from the school (Williams & Martin, 1922). The full text of the Creed reads: "I believe in the profession of journalism. I believe that the public journal is a public trust; that all connected with it are, to the full measure of their responsibility, trustees for the public; that acceptance of a lesser service than the public service is betrayal of this trust. I believe that clear thinking and clear statement, accuracy and fairness are fundamental to good journalism. I believe that a journalist should write only what he holds in his heart to be true. I believe that suppression of the news, for any consideration other than the welfare of society, is indefensible. I believe that no one should write as a journalist what he would not say as a gentleman; that bribery by one's own pocketbook is as much to be avoided as bribery by the pocketbook of another; that individual responsibility may not be escaped by pleading another's instructions or another's dividends. I believe that advertising, news and editorial columns should alike serve the best interests of readers; that a single standard of helpful truth and cleanness should prevail for all; that the supreme test of good journalism is the measure of its public service. I believe that the journalism which succeeds best — and best deserves success — fears God and honors Man; is stoutly independent, unmoved by pride of opinion or greed of power, constructive, tolerant but never careless, self-controlled, patient, always respectful of its readers but always unafraid, is quickly indignant at injustice; is unswayed by the appeal of

privilege or the clamor of the mob; seeks to give every man a chance and, as far as law and honest wage and recognition of human brotherhood can make it so, an equal chance; is profoundly patriotic while sincerely promoting international good will and cementing world-comradeship; is a journalism of humanity, of and for today's world."

8 Following a review of the research literature about constructive journalism and associated concepts, such as solutions journalism, Karin McIntyre and Keyser Lough write that the journalistic compass "offers opportunity for deeper theoretical linking between related forms in future research. If scholars consistently define these news forms using this model as a guide, they will bring consistency to the conceptualization of these approaches. Utilizing the journalistic compass can increase conceptual consistency" (McIntyre & Lough, 2021).

9 The journalistic compass has formerly been known under other names, such as the News Compass and the Action Compass (Bro, 2008).

10 This definition of constructive journalism is presented on the Constructive Institute's website (https://constructiveinstitute.org – accessed March 1, 2023).

11 One such example of persons and organizations using different names they believe are more precise is the "problem-solving reporting" done by a subdivision of the Danish Broadcasting Corporation. One of its premier practitioners has noted that "problem-solving journalism is a key that opens the door to following up on a good story. Problem-solving journalism rests on two basic pillars: the first, many goal-oriented follow-ups, and the second is a commitment to contribute towards problem solving by the use of a journalism" (Jesper Borup cf. Gyldensted, 2015, 115).

12 The three pillars of constructive journalism are presented on the Constructive Institute's website (https://constructiveinstitute.org – accessed March 1, 2023).

References

Ahva, Laura and Mikka Hautakangas (2018a) "Constructive forms in journalism [Special issue]." *Journalism Practice* 12 (6): 657–798.

Ahva, Laura and Mikka Hautakangas (2018b) "Introducing a new form of socially responsible journalism: Experiences from the conciliatory project." *Journalism Practice* 12 (6): 730–746

Andreassen, Andreas Marckmann (2010) "Mediechefer Kritiserer Ideen om 'Konstruktive Nyheder". "[Media Bosses Criticize the Notion of 'Constructive News']". *Journalisten*, November.

Barnhurst, Kevin G. and John Nerone (2001) *The Form of News*. New York: Guildford Press.

Benesch, Susan (1998) "The rise of solutions journalism." *Columbia Journalism Review* 36 (6): 36.

Bro, Peter (2008) "Normative navigation in the news media." *Journalism* 9 (3): 309–329.

Bro, Peter (2018) *Models of Journalism: The Function and Influencing Factors*. London: Routledge.

Bro, Peter (2019) "Constructive journalism: Principles, precedents, and practices." *Journalism* 20 (4): 504–519.

Campbell, W. Joseph (2001) *Yellow Journalism: Puncturing the Myths, Defining the Legacies*. London: Praeger.

Carey, James W. (1987) "The press and public discourse." *The Center Magazine* 20: 4–16.

Carey, James W. (1992/1975) "A cultural approach to communication." In *Communication as Culture*, edited by James W. Carey, 13–36, New York: Routledge.
Chalaby, Jean K. (2000) "Northcliffe's journalism." *Media History* 6 (1): 33–44.
Farrar, Ronald T. (1998) *A Creed for My Profession: Walter Williams, Journalist to the World.* Columbia: University of Missouri Press.
From, Unni and Nete Nørgaard Kristensen (2018) "Rethinking constructive journalism by means of service journalism." *Journalism Practice* 12 (6): 714–729.
Gyldensted, Cathrine (2011) *Innovating News Journalism Through Positive Psychology.* Master's Thesis, University of Pennsylvania.
Gyldensted, Cathrine (2012) "Spøgelset fra watergate – Nixon ud af nyhederne" [The ghost from Watergate – Nixon out of the news]. In *En Konstruktiv Nyhed* [A Constructive News Story], edited by Ulrik Haagerup, 185–198, Århus: Ajour.
Gyldensted, Cathrine (2015) *From Mirrors to Movers: Five Elements of Positive Psychology in Constructive Journalism.* Charleston, SC: Group Publishing.
Gyldensted, Cathrine and Malene Bjerre (2014) *Håndbog i konstruktiv Journalistic* [Handbook in Constructive Journalism]. Århus: Ajour.
Haagerup, Ulrik (2008) "Konstruktive nyheder" [Constructive News]. *Politiken*, December 6.
Haagerup, Ulrik (2012a) *En Konstruktiv Nyhed* [A Constructive News Story]. Århus: Ajour.
Haagerup, Ulrik (2012b) "Vejen frem" [The Road Ahead]. In *En konstruktiv Nyhed* [A Constructive News Story], edited by Ulrik Haagerup, 217–236, Århus: Ajour.
Haagerup, Ulrik (2014) *Constructive News: How to Save the Media and Democracy with Journalism of Tomorrow.* New York: InnoVatio Publishing.
Haagerup, Ulrik (2017) *Constructive News: How to Save the Media and Democracy With Journalism Of Tomorrow.* Aarhus, Denmark: Aarhus University Press.
Haslebo, Gitte and Magnus Haslebo (2010) *Nye Veje for Journalistikken* [New Roads for Journalism]. København: Dansk Psykologisk Forlag.
Hermans, Liesbeth and Nico Drok (2018) "Placing constructive journalism in context." *Journalism Practice* 12 (6): 679–694.
Hermans, Liesbeth and Tineke Prins (2020) "Interest matters: The effects of constructive news reporting on Millennials' emotions and engagement." *Journalism* 23 (5): 1064–1081.
Holmaas, Vigdis (2019) *Konstruktiv Journalistikk.* Bergen: Fakbokforlaget.
Jørgensen, Kristina Lund and Jakob Risbro (2021) *Konstruktiv Journalistik: Fra ide til Historie* [Constructive Journalism: From Idea to Story]. Århus: Forlaget Ajour.
Kovach, Bill and Tom Rosenstiel (2014/2001) *The Elements of Journalism: What News People Should Know and the Public Should Expect.* New York: Three Rivers Press.
Krüger, Uwe, Markus Beiler, Thilko Gläßgen, Michael Kees and Maximilian Küstermann (2022) "Neutral observers or advocates for societal transformation? Role orientation of constructive journalists in Germany." *Media and Communication* 10 (3): 64–77.
Lough, Kyser and Karen McIntyre (2019) "Visualizing the solution: An analysis of the images that accompany solutions-oriented news stories." *Journalism* 20 (4): 583–599.
Lough, Kyser and Karen McIntyre (2021) "A systematic review of constructive and solutions journalism research." *Journalism.* Advance Online Publication.

Mast, Jelle, Roel Coesemans and Martina Temmerman (2019) "Constructive journalism [Special issue]." *Journalism* 20 (4): 489–631.

May, Gerd Maria (2020) *Fra Tårn Til Torv* [From Tower to Square]. Odense: Syddansk Universitetsforlag.

McIntyre, Karen (2015) *Constructive Journalism: The Effects of Positive Emotions and Solution Information in News Stories*. Doctoral Dissertation, University of North Carolina, Chapel Hill, NC.

McIntyre, Karen, and Nicole Smith Dahmen (2021) *Reporting Beyond the Problem: From Civic Journalism to Solutions Journalism*. New York: Peter Lang.

McIntyre, Karen and Cathrine Gyldensted (2017) "Constructive journalism: Applying positive psychology techniques to news production." *The Journal of Media Innovations* 4 (2): 20–34.

McIntyre, Karen and Kyser Lough (2021) "Toward a clearer conceptualization and operationalization of solutions journalism". *Journalism* 22 (6): 1558–1573.

Pulitzer, Joseph (1904) *The School of Journalism at Columbia University*. New York: Columbia University Press.

Schudson, Michael (1995/1994) "Question authority: A history of the news interview." In *The Power of News*, edited by Michael Schudson, 72–93, Cambridge, MA: Harvard University Press.

Schudson, Michael (1995) "The news media and the democratic process." In *The Power of News*, edited by Michael Schudson, 204–223, Cambridge, MA: Harvard University Press.

Skovsgaard, Morten and Peter Bro (2017) "Journalistic roles in the mediated public sphere." In *Journalistic Role Performance: Concepts, Contexts, and Methods*, edited by Claudia Mellado, Lea Hellmueller and Wolfgang Donsbach, 60–74, London: Routledge.

Thier, Kathryn, Jesse Abdenour, Brent Walth and Nicole Smith Dahmen (2019) "A narrative solution: The relationship between solutions journalism, narrative transportation, and news trust." *Journalism* 22 (10): 2511–2530.

Wiener, Joel H. (2011) *The Americanization of the British Press, 1830s–1914*. London: Palgrave.

Williams, Walter and Frank L. Martin (1922/1911) *The Practice of Journalism*. Columbia: Missouri Book Services.

2 Precedents of constructive journalism

The history of journalism is characterized by continual development of new forms, formats, and platforms for journalism. The physical transportation of news stories – by foot, horseback, pigeon wings, locomotives, automobiles, and airplanes (see, e.g., Chalaby, 1998; Rantanen, 2009) – has been supplemented and often substituted with new, infinitely faster transmission technologies. From the optical telegraphy of the eighteenth century, where signposts were placed strategically throughout landscapes, to the electromagnetic telegraphy and lightning-fast digital technologies, the communication of news has experienced what some scholars refer to as "gearshifts" (Lash & Urry, 2002). Today, news stories can be produced, published, and distributed almost instantaneously, so they are experienced by news consumers while they unfold before the eyes of news producers. This diachronic approach, where journalism is viewed as a long succession of developments, rightly describes much of what has happened to the field of journalism, and to this day, new forms, formats, and platforms continue to develop – often at an astonishing speed in our digital era.

Another approach to the history of journalism focuses on the development of journalistic *ideologies*. When studying the history of journalism in a synchronic perspective, it becomes clear that the intentions, ideals, and ideas of journalists might well change over centuries and decades, over continents and countries, but these changes are often cyclic. That is, some ideals of what journalists and journalism should do seem to first appear, then disappear, only to reappear again. Such cyclic movements in media history are certainly evident when it comes to active types of journalism. As this chapter will show, journalists, editors, and owners of news organizations have repeatedly come up with the idea that news should do more than simply present problems. Indeed, the belief that journalists should actively move the world might have waned and waxed over the nineteenth, twentieth, and twenty-first centuries, but it has been part and parcel of journalism from the birth of modern journalism in the late nineteenth century.

This chapter describes the most important precedents of constructive journalism and discusses the similarities and the inherent internal differences

DOI: 10.4324/9781003403098-2

18 *Precedents of constructive journalism*

between what has been described over the last 150 years as "new journalism," "journalism that acts," "action journalism," "public journalism," "civic journalism," "community journalism," and "solutions journalism," just to mention some of the better-known labels that journalists, editors, and owners of news organizations have come up with. The long list of concepts is testament to several important points that will be addressed in this chapter, including the fact that constructive journalism has a long history, has been promoted by some of the most iconic figures in journalism, and continues to reappear in newsrooms around the world only to disappear again for a time. Why such attempts to do more than simply present problems have not taken root in newsroom in the past is also discussed in this chapter.

The new journalism of the nineteenth century

"New Journalism" was one of William Randolph Hearst's favorite explanations of his newspapers' success at the turn of the last century. The concept had been used before, most notably in the UK in the mid-1880s from where Hearst picked it up (Campbell, 2006, 42), and it was later reintroduced to describe the works of Tom Wolfe, Hunter S. Thompson, and other reporters, who in the 1960s and 1970s took to writing in a literary, subjective style.[1] But for Hearst, the notion of new journalism was well suited to distance his flagship newspaper, *The New York Journal*, from some of his rivals in the late nineteenth century. The perhaps most noteworthy competitor was *The New York Times*, which in 1896 was acquired by Adolph Ochs and practiced a more restrained type of journalism epitomized in Ochs's famous slogan "All the News That's Fit to Print."[2] Hearst did not refrain from belittling his competitors' practice of what he termed "old journalism," while he insistently boasted about the accomplishments of his owns newspapers, and testaments to his triumphs were often published on the front page and above the center fold in *The Journal*.

What this new journalism entailed was for a period summarized in a boxed slogan on the front page of *The Journal*, where the letters in the motto were almost as big as the name of the paper itself: "While others talk, The Journal acts." While it could be difficult for some readers to ascertain what the slogan at the masthead of the *New York Times* implied, Hearst, his editors, and journalists did not leave it to the readers' imagination to find out what *The Journal*'s slogan meant and what implications was carried with it. They practiced active journalism on a daily basis, and following a front-page appraisal of *The Journal*'s own work in 1897, the newspaper offered a more elaborate explanation to its readers:

> Action – that is the distinguishing mark of the new journalism. It represents the final stage in the evolution of the modern newspaper of a century

ago – the "new journals" of their day – told the news, and some of them made great efforts to get it first. The new journal of to-day prints the news too, but it does more. It does not wait for things to turn up. It turns them up.
(*The Journal*, October 13, 1897)

On this occasion, *The Journal* celebrated one of its own successful attempts at "turning things up," but "setting things free" might have been a better way of describing it. In the preceding days, editors and reporters at *The Journal* had orchestrated, organized, and eventually carried out a jailbreak in Cuba. Local authorities had incarcerated the daughter of a Cuban insurgent leader with strong U.S. ties, and working with local supporters, three reporters from *The Journal* had helped liberate the daughter, Evangeline Cisneros, by blowing up part of the federal prison building. In the following days, while the authorities conducted house-to-house searches in Havana, the reporters managed to smuggle the young woman on board a US-bound ship, and when Evangeline Cisneros a few days later arrived safely in New York City, *The Journal* retold the story on the front page with a pullout quote that boasted: "The journalism that does things." As if that was not enough, Hearst and *The Journal* also hosted a celebration on Times Square in New York City.

The Cisneros affair was, to be sure, one of the most spectacular – and widely discussed – examples of how *The Journal* could turn things up. It was definitely not fit for print, in the minds of many of Hearst's rivals and the political establishment, who all feared what the prison break might lead to. Everything from the end of diplomatic relations to an all-out war was mentioned. *The Journal* described its accomplishment as an "epochal moment" and a "supreme achievement," but the affair is testament to the belief of Hearst – and other prominent journalists, editors, and owners of news organizations of the time – that journalism could and should do more than simply report problems. "May a newspaper properly do things, or are its legitimate function confined to talking about them? That is the chief question at issue between the representatives of the new and the old journalism," another front-page piece in *The Journal* stated, before Hearst went on to describe his preference for, what he also described as a "journalism that acts," a "journalism of action," an "active journalism," an "action journalism," and even a "theory" and a "model" for journalism. For Hearst, his so-called theory meant that "a newspaper's duty is not confined to exhortation, but that when things are going wrong it should itself set them right, if possible," and he explained that "*The Journal* holds the theory that a newspaper may fitly render any public service within its power."

While Hearst was certainly one of the leading exemplars of active journalism at the turn of the last century, he was not alone in promoting and prompting "journalism that acts." Joseph Pulitzer was another prominent pioner and practitioner of what has since been described as an "activist paradigm" (Campbell, 2006), and he was the only other newspaper owner in the US who at the time could rival Hearst's commercial success. Over the years, Pulitzer amassed several newspapers on the American east coast, and at the height of its popularity, his New York-based newspaper, *The New York World*, sold more than 600,000 copies a day. Pulitzer was also a staunch supporter of newspapers taking a greater responsibility for what he often described as "the public welfare," and *The World* combated a broad variety of societal problem by regularly calling upon politicians, public authorities, and the public to act. Corruption, sickness, crime, poverty, and misuse of public funds were just some of the problems that journalist and editors at *The World* did their best to help solve. Some problems required the newspaper to prompt action among authoritative decision-makers, such as politicians, police commissioners, and company executives; other problems were solved by asking the public to donate money, material, or even their spare time.

Pulitzer's active journalism also took on other forms, and one of the most famous and lasting results of *The World*'s active journalism was the erection of the Statue of Liberty on Ellis Island, just south of New York City. "We must raise the money," Pulitzer wrote in *The World* (1885), when he became aware of financial problems. His plea for public assistance to – literally – raise the Statue of Liberty resulted in what has since been described as one of the most successful campaigns in U.S. history (Ware, 1938). More than 125,000 people contributed money for a pedestal, and Pulitzer later published the name of every known donor in his newspaper. Active journalism also took on other forms and was used, for example, to tear down things. One of *The World*'s most famous journalists, Nellie Bly, exposed the problems at a New York mental asylum after managing to get herself admitted and working undercover. Bly essentially broke into what was by her own later accounts comparable to a prison, and as a result of her reports, the asylum was eventually torn down.

While some of Bly's later journalistic work had a more entertaining form – like it happened when she traveled around the world in less than 80 days in order to emulate the travels of Jules Verne's fictional character Phileas Fogg – Bly was since heralded as one of the first so-called muckrakers.[3] Muckrakers were reform-minded journalists in the late nineteenth and the early twentieth century, who worked to expose corruption, crime, and other types of wrongdoing, and while muckrakers are forebearers of today's investigative journalists, it is important in this context to note that muckrakers worked in the belief that their reporting could help solve some of society's most pressing problems. The title of Judith Serrin and William Serrins's book about this period and journalist approach is telling of their accomplishments at the turn of the last century: *Muckraking: The Journalism That Changed America* (2002). While many contemporary journalists, editors, and others were critical of this approach and at times debunking it as "stunt journalism" and "crusading" the work of Bly and her colleagues – mostly men, it should be noted – also led to significant social, political, and economic reforms in the US in this period.

Such active attempts at making the world a better place by way of news reporting were not only practiced on the North American continent. Pulitzer, Hearst, and other American colleagues and competitors had originally been inspired by and embraced the concept of "new journalism" from England. Here, prominent editors and media owners such as William T. Stead, George Newness, and Alfred Harmsworth – later known as Lord Northcliffe – also experimented with active journalism.[4] Stead is of particular interest here, since he wrote a number of influential essays about the roles and responsibility of journalism. In 1883, Stead became the editor of *The Pall Mall Gazette* – a forerunner of *The London Evening Standard* – where he helped introduce many new *forms* of news (maps, diagrams, subheadings, etc.) and also sought to bring about new *norms* for what newspapers should do. In a seminal essay, "Journalism as Government" from 1886, Stead compared what he described as the "fourth estate" to the "all the other estates of the realm" and "branches of government," and he concluded that newspapers were superior to all of them when it came to ensuring public deliberations and subsequent actions to help society solve its problems.

In a key passage, Stead wrote about the importance of those journalists who had replaced politicians, scholars, and other professions, who had previously worked at newspapers and manned the desks in the newsrooms:

> A journalist can not only exercise an almost absolute power of closure both upon individuals and upon causes, he has also the power of declaring urgency for subjects on which he is interested. He can excite interest, or allay it; he can provoke public impatience, or convince people that no one need worry themselves about the matter. Every day he can administer either a stimulant or a narcotic to the minds of his readers.
>
> (Stead, 1886)

Stead conceded that the burgeoning profession of journalists was still unaware of its potential importance. "The very conception of journalism as an instrument of government is foreign to the mind of most journalists," he wrote, and the development of the UK press in the following years did not strengthen his hope for the future of "journalism as government." But when Stead learned of what took place across the Atlantic, and how people like Hearst had become inspired by the new journalism, he reached out to Hearst:

> I have been long on the look out for a man to appear who will carry out my ideal of government by journalism. I am certain that such a man will come to the front some day, and I wonder if you are to be that man.

Stead later visited the American media magnate in New York City, and when writing about "Mr. Hearst's famous definition of the difference between journalism that does things and the journalism that only chronicles them," Stead noted that Hearst had "grasped the idea, not perfectly but still resolutely, of government by journalism, and when experience and age have brought a little more steadiness Mr. Hearst may become the most powerful journalist in the world".

The exchange of idea about the responsibility and roles of journalism also left its mark on Hearst, and at the height of his success, he wrote that "newspapers, hardly less than a government, is the guardian of the people's rights," as he phrased it with reference to Stead's ideas in a column in *The World* entitled "A Newspaper's Duty to the Public" (1897). This idea of newspapers – in the hands of journalists – taking greater responsibility for the welfare of the public also caught on elsewhere, and on the European continent, several newspapers around the turn of the last century considered active journalism the most important of all journalistic approaches (Campbell, 2001). Another European supporter was the Danish journalist and editor, Henrik Cavling, who has been heralded for ushering in modern journalism in Denmark and for being an inspiration to other Nordic countries. Cavling took active journalism to heart after visiting the newsroom of *The Journal*. This visit was a source of inspiration that he wrote about in a travel book, *From America* (1897), and when the newspaper Cavling ran celebrated its 25th anniversary, he explained to readers that action journalism would define the future of journalism.

Cavling's proclamation coincides, almost verbatim, with Hearst's prediction a few years earlier. "(T)he final stage in the evolution of the modern journalism," Hearst wrote to readers on the front page of *The Journal*, contemplating the future importance of the new journalism that acts rather than simply "reacts." Cavling was more cautious, but when the newspaper he edited and directed – coincidentally the same newspaper where Ulrik Haagerup almost a century later published the column that first introduced the concept of constructive news to a wider public – celebrated its anniversary, Cavling noted:

> And it is on this relationship, which is still only at its beginning, that the magazine's development will largely depend. Journalism has planted its banner at the most opposite poles of the globe, and one might think that then there was no more new land for it to conquer. But action journalism opens up new and unlimited territories for the papers. A modern magazine, which can rightly say that nothing human is alien, finds everywhere it looks full of tasks.
>
> (Cavling, October 1, 1909)

Pulitzer was less vocal about his belief in action journalism, but he was perhaps the most expressive of them all about the importance of actively servicing the public. Following a lengthy essay in which Pulitzer stated that "public service" is "the ultimate end" for journalism (1904), he endowed a large part the money he had amassed over the years to the establishment of the journalism school at Columbia University and to the foundation of what was later referred to as the Pulitzer Prizes. The first initiative would help train future generations of journalists in classrooms to provide "public service," while the latter would reward those already working in newsrooms who managed to do just that. Upon his death, Pulitzer was praised for having been a constructive factor in society by way of his newspapers in New York City and St. Louis and for possessing "a peculiar constructiveness that was his own, and which had an influence on journalism throughout the country," as one obituary noted (cf. Bro, 2019).

Throughout the twentieth century, William Randolph Hearst, Joseph Pulitzer, William Stead, Lord Northcliffe, Henrik Cavling, and other proponents of active journalism certainly made their mark, and as Joseph Campbell has noted, active journalism was "easily the most promising" (2006, 107) of the models of journalism that evolved at the start of modern journalism in the 1890s. "It was *The Journal*'s vision, and not that of *The Times*, which appeared more likely to prevail, to win acceptance as the model for American journalism in the twentieth century" (2006, 107). Editors on the European continent also believed that active journalism would be the model on which journalism would and should develop. Things did not turn out that way, however, and it was to take almost another hundred years before the active journalism once again gained popularity in newsrooms around the world.

Public journalism of the twentieth century

There were several attempts at reviving and reinstituting more active approaches in journalism over the twentieth century. One of the more successful attempts was peace journalism, which developed in the 1960s and 1970s. The concept was originally introduced by Johan Galtung, a Norwegian peace researcher, who might be best known today among journalistic practitioners and researchers for his seminal study of the news values that guide journalists' decisions about what to make into news. In the article "The Structure of Foreign News" (1965), Galtung and Marie Ruge, also a peace researcher, suggested that 12 so-called news values could help explain much of what was published in newspapers, but an important part of this article was overlooked. Many practitioners, lecturers, and researcher have used the news values as a "model for" – something that journalists should strive to highlight in their news work – but Galtung and Ruge actually warned against just that near the end of their article.

Fearing what a constant focus on conflicts, crises, and other problems could produce in the minds of the audience – private citizens and political, military, and other decision-makers – Galtung, Ruge, and others suggested developing what was ultimately termed "peace journalism." "Peace journalism tries to depolarize by showing the black and white of all sides, and to deescalate by highlighting peace and conflict resolution as much as violence,"

Johan Galtung later described this approach (2003, 179). The notion of peace journalism caught on with some journalist and editors on both sides of the Atlantic, and its popularity was in part helped by an era where pacifism thrived in many Western countries. Peace journalism never became a major movement, and it was not until the last decades of the twentieth century that active journalism once again gained traction in newsrooms and started a new, major movement on both sides of the Atlantic. This time, things originated in the US where the movement, which since became known under many different names such as public journalism, civic journalism, and community journalism, developed from the late 1980s.

It all started with a criticism – by practitioners and researchers – of the journalism that had developed over the century. James Carey, a frequently cited scholarly critic, accused journalists and journalism for being out of touch with the public and claimed that the craft had developed into "a journalism that justifies itself in the public's name, but in which the public plays no role, except as an audience" (1997, 247). Another critic was political commentator David Broder from *The Washington Post*. Following a presidential election campaign that critics believed had led to a historically low turnout of voters, Broder wrote in a column entitled "Democracy and the Press" (1990) that the news media had lost sight of what was important for the craft: "We have to reposition ourselves in the political process. We have to distance ourselves from the people we write about and move ourselves closer to the people we write for" (1990).

Some practitioners and researchers went further than simply pointing out problems and started searching for solutions. Among the scholars was Jay Rosen, who by his own accounts was directly inspired by Joseph Pulitzer's emphatic call for a new profession of "public journalists" (Rosen, 1994, 373). Rosen believed that journalism researchers themselves were to blame for not doing more than simply pointing to problems in journalism. "It is not clear that our theorizing contributes enough to the resolution or even the common understanding of those troubles," Rosen wrote (1994, 363) with reference to the problems with traditional types of journalism that were discussed emphatically in academic circles but never had much impact outside the conference rooms. Rosen therefore took to working with journalists, editors, and others who were experimenting with new approaches. One of them, Davis "Buzz" Merritt, editor-in-chief at *The Wichita Eagle* in Kansas, along with his editors and journalists, had started experimenting with new ways of activating the public in election coverage. In one experiment, "We the people," citizens were asked what political issues they would prefer elections to be about rather than being asked the usual question: "Who would you vote for if an election were held tomorrow?" *The Eagle* also arranged town hall meetings where citizens were invited to ask questions directly to politicians to help the public set the agenda for the upcoming election.

In the start of the 1990s, Rosen and Merritt met at a seminar, and the following years they wrote a number of publications, individually and collective, about news ways of engaging the public. These works included books with telling titles such as *Public Journalism: Theory and Practice* (Rosen & Merritt, 1994) and *Imagining Public Journalism: An Editor and Scholar Reflect on the Birth of an Idea* (Merritt & Rosen, 1995). Their ideas caught on in many newsrooms, and while many of the first experiments focused on new ways of covering political elections, attention was soon turned to more everyday issues, where private citizens were invited to take part in public deliberations about issues that had largely been left to politicians before. In one of the most frequently referenced public journalism projects – the *Akron Beacon Journal*'s project "A Question of Color" – the newspaper worked to eradicate racial tensions. The project ran for ten months, resulted in 30 articles that appeared in five installments, and in the words of one researcher "the *Beacon Journal* tried to involve citizens in efforts to improve race relations by offering practical solutions to many of the problems examined and by helping to establish a local civic organization, the 'Coming Together Project'" (Haas, 2007, 84–85).

The project went on to win the 1994 Pulitzer Prize in Public Service – and it was in many ways a perfect extension of the active journalism that Pulitzer promoted in his newspapers. The project was heralded by the Pulitzer committee "for its broad examination of local racial attitudes and its subsequent effort to promote improved communication in the community." In some of the many examples of public journalism that began to spread throughout the country, improved communication – or deliberation as it was often described with reference to scholarly influences like John Dewey and Jürgen Habermas[5] – was an end in itself. "Information is what we have, deliberation is what we need," as Rosen mentioned at one point. But often the deliberations were thought of as a means to an end, since many of the projects involved efforts to help solve problems. "Journalism is in the problem-solving business," one of the most outspoken supporters of the news movement, Cole C. Campbell, editor of *St. Louis Post-Dispatch* (1999, xiv), put it after having experimented for almost a decade, while Merritt proclaimed that journalists should move beyond presenting news and become "fair-minded participants" in helping society prosper.

Another early promoter of the public journalism movement was *The Charlotte Observer*, and among its best-known projects were "The People Project: Solving It Ourselves" from 1992 and "Taking Back Our Neighborhoods" from 1994. The latter started with a front-page confession: "Virtually every poll in America puts crime at the top of citizens' concerns, but news coverage gets us nowhere and tends to frighten and depress readers," the editor-in-chief (Buckner cf. Charity, 1995) wrote, before she went on to announce a several month-long project, where the newspaper – together with a local television station and two local radio stations – actively attempted to mobilize its readers, viewers, and listeners to combat crime and violence in the 20th largest city in the US. "Taking Back Our Neighborhoods" started out by detailing concrete problems by analyzing local crime statistics, and after identifying the ten neighborhoods with the highest crime rates, the media partners started breaking down the problems, searching for solutions, and asking the public to assist. The results from one designated neighborhood is telling of the approach: reporters spent six weeks in a part of Charlotte known locally as "Seversville," where they talked to people about crime, its causes, consequences, and what might be done. The media partners also arranged two public meetings, and all of the initiatives resulted in a new Crime Watch unit, manned by residents, and a "needs page" that outlined what the neighborhood could do to combat rising crime, and what the city might do for this neighborhood (Rosen, 1999a).

One of the chroniclers of the public journalism movement, Arthur Charity, later wrote of this and the many other problem-solving projects that developed around the country:

> Acts of citizenship (besides voting) are unnecessarily hard for ordinary Americans to perform, and so, just as one ought to expect, they don't perform them often or well. They don't find common ground, draft clear messages, or act in concert to solve their problems. Journalists should always be on the lookout for ways to make those easier.
>
> (1995, 126)

Merritt, who initiated several public journalism projects, made a similar point in his books. "We need to see people not as readers, nonreaders, or endangered readers; not as customers to be wooed or an audience to be entertained; not as spectators at an event, but as a public, as citizens capable of action", he wrote in *Public Journalism and Public Life* (1995a, 80). At the end of the 1990s, another of the movement's main protagonists, Jay Rosen, summarized what the preceding century had amounted to in terms of election projects and special reporting projects by stating that public journalism is an approach to the daily business of the craft that calls on journalists to

> (1) address people as citizens, potential participants in public affairs, rather than victims or spectators; (2) help the political community act upon, rather than just learn about, its problems; (3) improve the climate of public discussion, rather than simply watch it deteriorate; and (4) help make public life go well, so that it earns its claim on our attention.
>
> (Rosen, 1999b, 22)

By then it was estimated that roughly half of all American newspapers, and radio and television stations had experimented with public journalism (Sirianni & Friedland, 2001), and the collective efforts were described as the "best organized social movement in the history of the American press" (Schudson, 1999, 118). Some news organizations promoted their accomplishment in public journalism projects and referred to the adherence to public journalism as a badge of honor. The Gannett newspaper chain, for example, took out a front-page advertisement in a trade magazine, *Editor and Publisher*, to let the rest of the industry know about their involvement in the movement. "We believe in 'public journalism' – and have done it for years," they advertised (Glasser, 1999a, 5). Indeed, as some researchers have later suggested, the popularity of public journalism can in part be explained by the fact that it became a potent combination of idealism and commercialism (Bro, 2019, 509). This point has been exemplified several times, for example, by a newspaper executive who explained that public journalism could become "a possible meeting ground between public service traditions in the press and the business imperatives of a struggling industry" (cf. Rosen, 1993, 14).

The popularity of public journalism was also helped by the formation of institutions that could analyze projects and initiate new experiments with journalists, editors, and owners of news organizations. Examples include the Center for Public Life and Public Journalism at New York University, directed by Jay Rosen and funded by foundations, and the Center for Civic Journalism located in Washington DC. Both worked actively to study new experiments, inspire future projects, and foster dialogue between practitioners and researchers with an interest in the movement, either because they supported the basic idea of public journalism or because they had a scholarly interest in the movement. At the turn of the last century, it was estimated that some 15 books and numerous research articles and articles in professional and trade journals in the news industry had been written (Zelizer, 2019). By then, the public journalism movement had also caught on in many other countries.

Another chronicler of the movement, Tanni Haas, traced public journalism projects to Africa (Malawi, Senegal, Swaziland), the Asia/Pacific Rim (Australia, Japan, New Zealand), Europe (Denmark, Finland, Sweden), and South America (Argentina, Columbia, Mexico) (2007). As public journalism spread to newsrooms and classrooms around the world, however, it became increasingly clear that it was being practiced in many different ways. Some of these practices seemed at odds with each other, and just a few years into the new century, the concept lost its hold on practitioners and researchers, and supporters stopped referring to it.[6] Interestingly, several of the practices developed as part of the movement for a more public journalism became integral parts of traditional journalism – just as it happened a century earlier when many of the new forms of journalism survived, the new norms of journalism they originally had been introduced to help serve. The most famous example from the public journalism era is perhaps agenda-setting polls, which asked private citizens to decide which political issues journalists should cover during elections (Bro, 2019). However, public journalism came to resemble the movement a century earlier, and in the first years of the twenty-first century support for the public journalism movement and the concept itself withered away.

The constructive journalism of the twenty-first century

At the peak of public journalism's popularity, some scholars pointed to the similarities between this new movement and the movement a hundred years prior. Michael Schudson considered public journalism the "perfect extension" (1999, 123) of the progressive era around the turn of the last century when private citizens were considered important social actors who should be included in public affairs. Thomas Leonard has also noted this shared attempt to include private citizens in public affairs and has described the active movement in the late nineteenth century as a "(p)recursor of public journalism" (1999, 87). But as Joseph Campbell has rightly noted, there is an even "more central connection" (2001, 180) between the two periods than these attempts to include private citizens, and he has more specifically pointed to "the problem-solving ethic that was central to both" movements (2001, 180). Those historical contingencies were not considered and factored in as public journalism developed.

The name of the movement in the late twentieth century might have been inspired by Joseph Pulitzer's call for public journalists, but the proponents were criticized for exhibiting a problematic "ahistoricism" (Zelizer, 2019, 158). While people like Jay Rosen and Davis Merritt offered a compelling criticism of the immediate past, they and others failed to make it clear for both supporters and opponents how their suggested solutions to current problems related directly to some of the oldest and most foundational principles of the craft. This opportunity was not missed by the new movement that developed in the twenty-first century. In the case of constructive journalism, the historical connections to prior movements and classic journalistic principles were built in from the beginning by the new movement's primary proponents, Ulrik Haagerup and Cathrine Gyldensted. Even if they and later supporters and promotors might not have fully thought these historical connections through, and the first works about constructive journalism only mentioned them in a cursory fashion.

In his first monograph – in Danish – Haagerup points specifically to constructive journalism's antecedents in the 1990s. In a section about historical roots, he notes, "The experiments had names like public journalism, civic journalism, solutions journalism, citizens' journalism, and many other terms—all with the intention to promote more problem-solving reporting" (2014, 67). Gyldensted goes even further back and points to the similarities with the progressive period around the turn of the nineteenth and twentieth centuries. In her first book about constructive journalism, *From Mirrors to Movers* (2015), Gyldensted recounts how another Dane, Jacob A. Riis, who immigrated from Denmark to the US in the late nineteenth century, became one of the best-known representatives of the social reformers of that era. Riis, who worked as a journalist and photographer in order to – literally – shine a light on the problems he believed should be corrected, was called the "the most useful citizen" by President Theodore Roosevelt (Ware, 1938, 78). Gyldensted notes that back then, journalism was also "shown to have a role in improving society" (2015, 6).

While constructive journalism – as opposed to the public journalism movement – has highlighted the earliest historical precedents, its beginning resembles that of the other two movements. Common to all three movements is their starting point: a criticism of the existing. In the case of constructive journalism, the main criticism of the existing journalism was not directed at a disconnect from or disservice to the public when it came to helping it solve its problems. Instead, criticism was directed at the "negativity bias" of the contemporary news media. In the very first column where Haagerup introduced the concept of "constructive news," he criticized traditional journalism for having an overly "negative" focus. In this and in many other contexts, Haagerup has openly acknowledged that this focus has been an integral part of his professional career and something he has imposed on other journalists. In *Constructive News* from 2017, for example, Haagerup recounts that he was taught in journalism school that "[a] good story is a bad story. If nobody gets mad, it's advertising" (2017, 13), and he explains how this approach since then ran "in his veins" (2017, 13).

Gyldensted has also based her call for constructive journalism on a criticism of the "negative" journalism, and according to both proponents, this focus is problematic for several reasons. One is content. Haagerup has made a point on several occasions of exemplifying this negativity slant by pointing to some of the news programs he has been in charge of. Indeed, this has at times become his signature approach of his. In the anthology from 2012, his introductory chapter with the telling title *A Constructive News Story: Showdown with the Press's Negative World View* (2012; published in Danish) recounts the rundown of an evening news program from the national public service broadcaster. The transcript starts with the introductory remarks by the anchor, who welcomes viewers, before listing the news stories that will be covered in the program. Headline after headline is mentioned, ending with a brief statement about the upcoming weather forecast.

The transcript in the book reads: "There are new terror threats against Denmark," "New shooting incident in Copenhagen," "New trains from problematic supplier," "Cervical cancer threatens young girls," "Strikes among taxi drivers continues," "Woman abused in shed in Sweden," "Crisis-stricken Social Democrats convene for congress," "Lawsuit after plane crash with hundreds killed," "20-kilo spider causes fear in Liverpool," "and then there is the weather: The grey weather continues" (Haagerup, 2012, 23). Gyldensted makes similar points in her works about the widespread focus in the news media on problems, and according to Gyldensted, Haagerup, and other critics who have since joined the constructive journalism movement, this content is problematic in itself because it factors out the positive aspects of life, *and* it may even affect audiences negatively.

Haagerup starts his column from 2008 with a reference to a personal encounter: "'It's pretty annoying,' said my friend's lanky daughter," after reading newspapers and watching TV news for a whole week as part of her homework. Something she feared, she admitted to Haagerup, since the news made it difficult for her to sleep. In the following lines, Haagerup mentions a host of other people he has met under professional or personal circumstances, and who all tend to confront him and journalists more generally with the question: "Why are you so negative?" Haagerup later used this question as headline of the opening chapter of his first book in English (2014). Gyldensted likewise refers to personal encounters, but her criticism of the effect of the news media is also based on her academic study of how people perceive the news.

After leaving journalism, Gyldensted took up graduate studies in positive psychology to learn from other fields and inspire new approaches to journalism. As part of her master's thesis, she conducted an experiment with 710 respondents who were asked to read six different versions of the same news stories with a framing that in the words of Gyldensted ranged from the "very positive" over the "classic" to the "very negative" (Gyldensted, 2012, 191). The study led her to conclude that a news story with a negative frame reduced positive emotions and increased negative emotions significantly (Gyldensted, 2011). Based on personal experiences and professional studies – and with references to, among others, psychologists who warn some of their clients to stop following the news, Gyldensted and Haagerup conclude in several of their publications that traditional news tends to depress the audience and may cause them to avoid the news altogether (see, e.g., Gyldensted, 2015; Haagerup, 2017).

However, the negativity bias also has other negative implications. On several occasions, Haagerup has pointed to the paradox that the more news people consume, the less they actually know about the state of the world. In *Constructive News* (2017), Haagerup points to research – for example, by the late Hans Rosling (2018) – that shows that the nature of news gives people a distorted and, by most accounts, overly negative view of, for example, crime, terror, diseases, poverty, and unemployment. To illustrate, at an international conference hosted by Constructive Institute, hundreds of attendees from the news industry, research institutions, and other societal sectors associated with journalism were asked in an instant, on-site survey to describe the state of the world and collectively proved generally more pessimistic than warranted by reality. Tellingly, a randomly assigned control group with a considerably lower news consumption than the attendees at the conference proved more knowledgeable.

Some critics believe that an even worse effect of problem-based journalism is that it has little or no effect. This is something that both Haagerup and Gyldensted focus on in their first publications. Their point is that they were both taught and trained to focus on societal problems in the belief that this would help solve those problems. "I am a journalist. I went into the profession … to do good for society," Haagerup writes in the introduction to *Constructive News* (2017, 13). He was inspired by other journalists and editors, most notably some of the famous investigative reporters from the second half of the twentieth century, practiced this approach and won prizes for his investigative reporting, including the most prestigious journalistic prize in Denmark, the Cavling Prize.

While the criticism of traditional journalism has taken many and varied directions, the core basically remains the same: the problem with journalism is its inherent focus on problems. The proponents of constructive journalism therefore suggested adding a focus on what might best be described as "potentials." Potentials can be defined as things that already works or could work well in the future – and as such help inspire others. When writing about these two approaches – a focus on problems or a focus on potentials – both Haagerup and Gyldensted have noted the need for supplementation rather than substitution, and they have expressed this duality in several ways. Gyldensted has mentioned a number of apparent opposites in her works, like "male and female," "hot and cold," and "summer and winter," and sums up that people, in general, need both. "Likewise with negative stories and constructive stories," she adds and explains that journalism needs both because "[t]ogether they portray the world accurately (2015, 8). This belief is shared by Haagerup:

> Constructive news criticizes traditional news journalism where you only see the world with one eye. It does not argue that it is better to just see it with the other eye. Instead, good journalism is seeing the world with both eyes.
>
> (Haagerup, 2014, 111)

Supplementing the two approaches would, according to Haagerup, lead to "the best obtainable version of the truth" (2017, 16), and this acceptance of the importance of traditional journalism has no doubt helped popularize constructive journalism in many newsrooms around the world. It is not a question of one or the other approach – "the tyranny of the or," as Haagerup (2008) explained when he introduced the concept of constructive news – and in many countries around the world journalists are now, occasionally or continuously, experimenting with constructive journalism. The result has, so far, been remarkable. This latest attempt to promote and prompt active journalism has in many ways come to rival the success of its predecessors in the nineteenth and twentieth centuries.

In the case of public journalism, centers and institutes were formed to pave the way for more research and innovations, like the Project on Public Life and the press at New York University, where Jay Rosen was director, and the Center for Civic Journalism based in Washington DC. In time, public journalism also became an object of study in hundreds of research articles and scores of books, and it was introduced in newsrooms and classrooms in many countries around the world. The same has happened to constructive journalism, and more and more monographs, anthologies, scholarly articles, and articles in trade magazines seem to be published each year (see, e.g., Lough & McIntyre, 2021). Centers and institutes have also been established. The Constructive Institute in Denmark, which Ulrik Haagerup founded in 2017 after he left his position as news director at the Danish Broadcasting Company, has been joined by others. A recent example is the Bonn Institute in Germany, established in 2022, which aims to spread knowledge about the principles and practice of constructive journalism. Constructive journalism has also become a topic at journalism school, and already back in 2015, Gyldensted was hired to organize the first ever program in constructive journalism, at Windesheim University in Holland. Since then, courses and classes in constructive journalism have been offered at an increasing number of journalism schools and universities.

The overall result of all of these initiatives has been that constructive journalism matches if not surpasses its predecessors as one of the fastest-growing and internationally widespread movements in the history of journalism. But for all of the success, constructive journalism has also come to resemble the movements in the nineteenth and twentieth centuries in another, more negative way, namely, the conceptual unclarity when it comes to what this type of journalism entails both in principle and in practice. First and foremost, there is the concept itself and what it means. The founders have, over the years, stressed several things. At times, Haagerup and Gyldensted have pointed to the importance of presenting news about what goes well in society. This is an approach that Gyldensted in her early works dubbed "positive journalism" (see, e.g., 2012, 2015). At other times, the two founders have pointed to the need for news that presents what could go well in the future and as such might offer solutions and inspiration (Bro, 2019).

This dual perspective is one of the things that differentiate constructive journalism from solutions journalism since the latter has a narrower focus. Karen McIntyre has rightly noted that "a solutions-based news story is constructive, but a constructive news story does not require the inclusion of a solution" (2015, 16). Things have not become much clearer over the years, and today constructive journalism seems to encompass even more things. Haagerup has introduced the pillars of constructive journalism: looking for solutions, embracing nuances, and engaging and facilitating the public in debate, where the latter introduces a new approach to the concept of constructive journalism. This is, incidentally, also a perspective that Gyldensted has included in her own, later works. In her latest book, *Did You Get Smarter: How to Improve Public Conversation* (2020), she introduces new formats for a better and more inclusive public debate. But things are even more complex when it comes to constructive journalism. For there is also a lack of clarity when it comes to how far constructive journalists should go in their attempt to be "movers" of the world to paraphrase the title of Gyldensted's first monograph.

In this book, Gyldensted differentiates between two approaches, the stick and the carrot. First, using the stick, journalism has "a role in improving society by exposing the negative sides of life" (2014, 6), she writes. Using the carrot, journalism "investigates opportunities, looks at dilemmas from all sides, and indicates remedies. It does not ignore the problems and it does not trivialize them; instead, it focuses on how these problems can be solved" (2014, 7). Gyldensted suggests that journalists in the future should add "more carrot while we kept the stick," since both approaches are useful for journalists who want to move the world. But she does not specify how active journalists should be, if their audience does not respond to either the stick or the carrot, and it is even more difficult to determine how active Haagerup thinks journalists should be in ensuring action by the public or its representatives.

Several of his publications contain statements that seem to run parallel with Gyldensted's. "How can we save journalism by helping it save the world," Haagerup writes in his first monograph (2014, 4) and adds that "good journalism can inspire the solutions to the problems facing society, giving way to a new and meaningful role for journalism" (2014, 4–5). On the other side, Haagerup is cautious about what a focus on solutions entails and what journalists' responsibilities are. In one of his later books, Haagerup writes about some of the misconceptions of constructive journalism he has encountered over the years. He refers to these as "booby traps," and one is labeled "Do not be a politician." According to Haagerup, constructive journalists will argue that

> A good story can be inspirational, and that journalism can facilitate a better public debate on possible solutions to the problems facing society. But it is not the job of any professional journalist to decide what the right solution is. That would be turning journalism into activism or pure politics.
> (2017, 141)

The question how active journalists should be in making the world a better place – by presenting problems, potentials, or other journalistic activities – remains one of the unresolved issues in constructive journalism.

The rise and fall of active journalism

The history of journalism shows us that three major movements have attempted to promote active types of journalism that do more than simply present problems. Some observers have rightly noted that there are other "branches," "sub-genres," and other "associated concepts" that could be worth mentioning when discussing constructive journalism. Karen McIntyre and Cathrine Gyldensted have, for example, pointed specifically to "peace journalism," "restorative narrative," "prospective journalism," "solutions journalism," and "positive journalism" in their article "Constructive Journalism: Applying Positive Psychology Techniques to News Production" (2017, 24). But with the exception of solutions journalism, none of these branches have found as receptive an audience in newsrooms around the world as three major movements described here. The three major movements in the history of journalism have, however, not been described consistently, and as this chapter has shown journalistic practitioners and researchers have used many different concepts and catchphrases over the years (see Figure 2.1)

The many concepts and catchphrases illustrate several important points. First, they have been used by proponents of each movement to help people, inside and outside newsrooms, differentiate between journalistic norms. The history of journalism thus reminds us that "like all practices, those of journalists are contingent; that is, they are variable over time, place, and circumstance," as James Carey has described it (1997, 331). This is important, as Carey has rightly emphasized, since nothing "disables journalists more than thinking that current practice is somehow in the nature of things" (1997, 331). It is culture rather than nature that determines how the forms and norms of journalism develop, and there is more than one way to do journalism. That said, the three movements – with their many names – illustrate a second important point, namely, that attempts to do more than simply present problems have been an undercurrent in journalism for several centuries, and active journalism has been held in high regard by generations of journalists, editors, and owners of news organizations – including some of the most iconic figures in journalism. In this sense, the many concepts and catchphrases are reminders that what people hold dear often goes under many names.

Figure 2.1 Concepts and catchphrases used to describe active types of journalism.

However, the many names also point to a third important point: the lack of authoritative accounts of what each movement entails. Common to the movements – in particular when it comes to the two latter – is that the proponents have offered a timely criticism of more traditional types of journalism that have received widespread support, both inside and outside newsrooms. For example, persons associated with the public journalism movement have collectively been heralded for stirring "the most impressive critique of journalistic practice inside journalism in a generation" (Schudson, 1999, 118), and the pioneers of constructive journalism have also helped spark debates and discussions about the nature of news even among those who have not believed that constructive journalism is the answer to these problems. But the proponents have been less precise about their own alternatives and in general have kept their definitions open. Whether by neglect or necessity, proponents, promoters, and supporters of each movement have never done enough to precisely define their own movements and delineate how they differ from other types of journalism.

From the first active movement in the late nineteenth century, they have been characterized by what researchers have described as a "definitional elusiveness" (Campbell, 2001, 6) and a "lexical elasticity" (Bro, 2019, 510). In the public journalism and constructive journalism movements, conceptual elusiveness and elasticity were encoded by design. In the case of constructive journalism, Haagerup and Gyldensted have deliberately chosen not to define their approaches narrowly. "Experiment with new ideas, new questions, new angles, and new ways. Find out what works, and what needs to be corrected," Haagerup suggested in *Constructive News* (2014, 113), and his Constructive Institute continues to engage in a wide variety of experiments. In *From Mirrors to Movers*, Gyldensted wrote that constructive journalism is "not a static domain but will evolve as the research underpinning method and application evolve" (2014, 174), and, as noted in the Introduction, she has maintained this position and continues to see "an organic domain, that will need to be revised, matured and progressed as we go along" (cf. Bro, 2019).

Statements such as these have much in common with the primary proponents of the public journalism movement. The "definitional elusiveness" was built into the movement from its inception as the early proponents insisted on keeping the definition open. "The most important thing anyone can say about public journalism, I will say right now: We're still inventing it. And because we're inventing it, we don't really know what 'it' is," Jay Rosen noted (1994, 388). Another proponent, Davis Merritt, considered it an "arrogant exercise, a limiting one to codify a set of public journalism rules" (1995, 124). This conceptual openness led one critic to wonder, "Is it a movement, a philosophy, or a model?" (Zelizer, 1999, 157). This criticism was raised in an anthology, *The Idea of Journalism* (Glasser, 1999b), and things were not made clearer when Rosen noted in a chapter that he considered public journalism to be "an argument," "an experiment," "a movement," "a debate," and "an adventure" (1999b, 22–23).

The third movement, which originated at the turn of the last century, suffered from the same problems, and, in hindsight, it is not surprising that the popularity of active journalism withered away in the first decades of the twentieth century. For one thing, the proponents were highly industrious and innovative people who experimented with many new norms and forms of journalism. The journalistic methods and modes of presentation developed and implemented by Hearst, Pulitzer, Harmsworth, Cavling, and others have been described as "revolutions," and Pulitzer, for one, has been described as the "foremost innovator of new journalism in America in the late nineteenth century" (Wiener, 2011, 155). However, some of the proponents of active journalism also stood in the way of its advancement. Both William Randolph Hearst and Joseph ran for political office. Pulitzer was a state representative in Missouri and elected to the U.S. House of representatives, and Hearst was elected twice to Congress and only narrowly failed to become governor and mayor of New York. This led to accusations of slanted journalism and doubt about the objectivity they had championed as servants of the public.

Hearst's and Pulitzer's political careers made people question their motives, when their newspapers worked to solve societal problems, and Hearst, in particular, was often accused of conflating political affairs with the affairs of his newspapers. In time, critics even introduced derogatory concepts to describe the active journalism, and the term "yellow journalism" has stuck. "Yellow journalism" was a comic strip introduced by *The World* and later acquired by *The Journal*. The protagonist of the strip was called the "yellow kid." While the names Hearst, Pulitzer, Stead, Cavling, and others have stood the test of time in journalism, the journalistic ideals they originally championed have been susceptible to misunderstandings. Likewise, the conceptual elasticity of public journalism has given way to myths, misunderstandings, and subsequent name-calling. One of the most debated statements about what public journalism actually was occurred when a former news executive proclaimed that the decision by *Washington Post* and *New York Times* to give in to pressure from the so-called "Unabomber" and publish a statement from him was an example of public journalism (Glasser, 1999a).

In some instances, the names have caused problems. As Barbie Zelizer has noted, "affixing the term 'public' to 'journalism' is a problematic linguistic ploy that activates an underlying tension in the profession". Her point is that by "making its own nominal claims to the public journalism essentially belittles all other types of journalism for not doing the same" (Zelizer, 1999, 161). The other categories suffer from the same problem. The "journalism-that-does-things" from the nineteenth century presupposes that other types of journalism do not accomplish anything of importance, and constructive journalism seems to suggest that other types of journalism might be destructive.

While the proponents have argued that the particular types of journalism, they promote, are simply intended to highlight the importance of what their names imply, the name giving has caused antagonism even among those who essentially support the idea that journalism should do more than present problems.

There are, to be sure, differences between the three movements that have promoted more active types of journalism in the nineteenth, twentieth, and twenty-first centuries. But the similarities are remarkable, and over time these three major journalistic movements have developed in much the same way. The conceptual elusiveness and elasticity play a pivotal role, for better and worse. On one side, open definitions have positive sides. As the proponents of the three movements have suggested, leaving things open can help innovation and experimentation and may popularize movements, since many critics of established journalism can rally and ally around these new approaches. On the other side, conceptual elusiveness is problematic. The history of journalism has shown how movements – even the ones spearheaded by journalistic icons – have gained popularity for a few years or decades, only to die out.

This criticism has been extended to encompass the latest movement, constructive journalism, which

> runs the risk of meeting the same fate as movements of the past, if its original proponents – or the practitioners, lectures, and researchers who have become inspired by it – do not offer stronger definitions and define the borders that separate it from other types of journalism.
>
> (Bro, 2019, 512)

Chapter 3, about the principles of constructive journalism, will describe and discuss the similarities and differences inherent in the concept of constructive journalism in hopes that it can lead to stronger definitions and define the borders that separate it from – and unites it with – other types of journalism.

Notes

1 New journalism has been used several times throughout the history of journalism to denote novel types of journalism, but today most people, inside and outside of journalism, might associate it with the movement, also known as "gonzo journalism," from the late twentieth century. Writers, such as Hunter S. Thompson, Tom Wolfe, and Norman Mailer, were known for their subjective perspectives and their use of literary techniques.

2 Michael Schudson and other observers of this period have suggested that the different approaches to these two types of journalism is best described as a "journalism as information" and a "journalism of entertainment" (1978). For Schudson, the first is exemplified by the *New York Times*, while the latter is best represented by the *World* and the *Journal*. The dichotomy has later been criticized for failing to consider the social, economic, political, and other reforms that Hearst, Pulitzer, and others attempted to bring about by way of the active journalism.

3 Nellie Bly was born Elisabeth Jane Cochran, but was given the pseudonym by the first editor she wrote for. Bly did manage to travel around the world faster that Jules Verne's fictional character, Phileas Fogg from the book *Around the World in Eighty Days*, that she was competing with. It took Bly 72 days to travel around the world, and she even found time to meet Jules Vernes on the tour.

4 Jean Chalaby (2000) differentiates between three "archtypical" crusades in the British Press: the social crusade, the jingo crusade, and the stunt crusades. He notes that Stead was among the first to develop such crusades and that he preferred the first two kinds, whereas Northcliffe often also made use of the third type of crusades.

5 Jay Rosen, at one time, offered what he described as the shortest definition of public journalism: "What Dewey meant" (1999b, 24). While the works of John Dewey and Jürgen Habermas did not matter much to the practitioners associated with the public journalism movement, they played an important part of the work done by Rosen and other researchers (see, e.g., Haas, 2007; Rosen, 1999a). Rosen found that Dewey's and Habermas's works could form the foundation of a new journalistic approach, where the public played a more direct role in society. For Dewey, the essential ambition was to ensure public deliberations where private citizens could come together, communicate, and coordinate actions.

6 In time, some journalistic practitioners and researchers started coming up with other concepts that they believed better encapsulated the essence public and civic journalism. Conversational journalism, community journalism, citizen journalism, solutions journalism, and solutions-based journalism are such examples, and in time, these concepts have gone on to have different meanings. Another example was when the Pew Center for Civic Journalism changed its name to the Institute for Interactive Journalism (Bro, 2019).

References

Bro, Peter (2019) "Constructive journalism: Principles, precedents, and practices." *Journalism* 20 (4): 504–519.

Broder, David (1990) "Democracy and the press." *Washington Post*, January 3.

Campbell, Cole C. (1999) "Foreword: Journalism as a democratic act." In *The Idea of Public Journalism*, edited by Theodore L. Glasser, xiii–xxix, New York: Guildford Press.

Campbell, W. Joseph (2001) *Yellow Journalism: Puncturing the Myths, Defining the Legacies*. London: Praeger.

Campbell, W. Joseph (2006) *The Year That Defined American Journalism: 1897 and the Clash of Paradigms*. New York: Routledge.

Carey, James W (1997) "Afterword: The culture in question." In *James Carey: A Critical Reader*, edited by Eve Stryker Munson and Cathrine A. Warren, 308–339, Minneapolis, MN: Minneapolis University Press.

Cavling, Henrik (1897) *Fra Amerika* [From America]. København: Gyldendalske Boghandels Forlag.

Cavling, Henrik (1909) "Bladet" [The Paper]. *Politiken*, October 1.

Chalaby, Jean K. (1998) *The Invention of Journalism*. London: Macmillan Press Ltd.

Chalaby, Jean K. (2000) "Northcliffe's journalism." *Media History* 6 (1): 33–44.

Charity, Arthur (1995) *Doing Public Journalism*. New York: Guildford Press.

Galtung, Johan (2003) "Peace journalism." *Media Asia* 30 (3): 177–180.

Galtung, Johan and Marie Ruge (1965) "The structure of foreign news." *Journal of Peace Research* 2 (1): 64–91.

Glasser, Theodore L, (1999a) "The idea of public journalism." In *The Idea of Public Journalism*, edited by Theodore L. Glasser, 3–18, New York: Guildford Press.

Glasser, Theodore L. (1999b) *The Idea of Public Journalism.* New York: Guilford Press.

Gyldensted, Cathrine (2011) *Innovating News Journalism through Positive Psychology.* Master's Thesis, University of Pennsylvania.

Gyldensted, Cathrine (2012) "Spøgelset fra Watergate – Nixon ud af nyhederne" [The ghost from Watergate – Nixon out of the news]. In *En Konstruktiv Nyhed* [A Constructive News Story], edited by Ulrik Haagerup, 185–198, Århus: Ajour.

Gyldensted, Cathrine (2015) *From Mirrors to Movers: Five Elements of Positive Psychology in Constructive Journalism.* Charleston, SC: Group Publishing.

Gyldensted, Cathrine (2020) *Blev du Klogere: Sådan Forbedrer du den Offentlige Samtale* [Did You Get Smarter: How to Improve Public Conversation]. København: Forlaget Højskolerne.

Haagerup, Ulrik (2008) "Konstruktive nyheder" [Constructive News]. *Politiken*, December 6.

Haagerup, Ulrik (2012) Et opgør med nyhedsvanen [A showdown with the news habit]. In *En konstruktiv Nyhed* [A Constructive News Story], edited by Ulrik Haagerup, 21–46, Århus: Ajour.

Haagerup, Ulrik (2014) *Constructive News: How to Save the Media and Democracy with Journalism of Tomorrow.* New York: InnoVatio Publishing.

Haagerup, Ulrik (2017) *Constructive News: How to Save the Media and Democracy with Journalism of Tomorrow.* Aarhus, Denmark: Aarhus University Press.

Haas, Tanni (2007) *The Pursuit of Public Journalism: Theory, Practice, and Criticism.* New York: Routledge.

Lash, Scott & John Urry (2002) *Economies of Signs and Space.* London: Sage.

Leonard, Thomas (1999) "Making readers into citizens – The old-fashioned way." In *The Idea of Public Journalism*, edited by Theodore Glasser, 85–96, New York: Guildford Press.

Lough, Kyser and Karen McIntyre (2021) "A systematic review of constructive and solutions journalism research." *Journalism.* Advance Online Publication.

McIntyre, Karen (2015) *Constructive Journalism: The Effects of Positive Emotions and Solution Information in News Stories.* Doctoral Dissertation, University of North Carolina, Chapel Hill, NC.

McIntyre, Karen and Cathrine Gyldensted (2017) "Constructive journalism: Applying positive psychology techniques to news production." *The Journal of Media Innovations* 4 (2): 20–34.

Merritt, Davis (1995a) *Public Journalism and Public Life.* Mahwah, NJ: Lawrence Erlbaum Associates.

Merritt, Davis and Jay Rosen (1995) *Imagining Public Journalism: An Editor and Scholar Reflect on the Birth of an Idea.* Bloomington: Roy W. Howard Project, School of Journalism, Indiana University.

Pulitzer, Joseph (1885) "We must raise the money." *The New York World*, March 16.

Rantanen, Terhi (2009) *When News was New.* West Sussex: Wiley-Blackwell.

Rosen, Jay (1993) *Community-Connectedness: Passwords for Public Journalism.* St. Petersburg: Poynter Institute for Media Studies.

Rosen, Jay (1994) "Making things more public: On the political responsibility of the media intellectual." *Critical Studies in Mass Communication* 11 (4): 363–388.

Rosen, Jay (1999a) *What Are Journalists for?* New Haven, CT: Yale University Press.

Rosen, Jay (1999b) "The action of the idea". In *The Idea of Public Journalism*, edited by Theodore L. Glasser, 21–48, New York: Guilford Press.

Rosen, Jay and Davis Merritt (1994) *Public Journalism: Theory and Practice*. Dayton, OH: Kettering Foundation.

Rosling, Hans (2018) *Factfulness: Ten Reasons We're Wrong About the World – and Why Things Are Better Than You Think*. New York: Flatiron Books.

Schudson, Michael (1978) *Discovering the News*. New York: Basic Books.

Schudson, Michael (1999) "What public journalism knows about journalism but doesn't know about 'public'." In *The Idea of Public Journalism*, edited by Theodore Glasser, 118–133, New York: Guilford Press.

Serrin, Judith and William Serrin (2002) *Muckraking: The Journalism that Changed America*. New York: The New Press.

Sirianni, Carmen and Lewis Friedland (2001) *Civic Innovation in America*. Berkeley: University of California Press.

Stead, William T. (1886) "Government by journalism." *The Contemporary Review* 49 (May): 653–674.

Ware, Louise (1938) *Jacob A. Riis, Police Reporter, Reformer, Useful Citizen*. New York: Appelton-Century Company.

Wiener, Joel H. (2011) *The Americanization of the British Press, 1830s–1914*. London: Palgrave.

Zelizer, Barbie (1999) "Making the neighborhood work: The improbabilities of public journalism." In *The Idea of Public Journalism*, edited by Theodore Glasser, 152–172, New York: Guilford Press.

3 Principles of constructive journalism

"Our Republic and its press will rise or fall together," starts one of the most referenced proclamations about the importance of journalism. Many people – also outside of journalism – know the name of the person who coined the statement, Joseph Pulitzer (1904, 48). Fewer know how the statement continues. Pulitzer makes an important distinction between a "cynical, mercenary, demagogic press" and an "able, disinterested, public-spirited press, with trained intelligence to know the right and courage to do it" (1904, 48). The former works as hired help to advance the viewpoints of political leaders, company executives, and other special interests, and "will produce in time a people as base as itself" (1904, 48). The latter could "preserve that public virtue without which popular government is a sham and a mockery" (1904, 48). Pulitzer ends the proclamation by leaving the choice between the two to the new profession for which he more than most paved the way: "The power to mould the future of the Republic will be in the hands of the journalists of future generations" (1904, 48).

The famous proclamation appeared in an essay, in which he makes a strong case for the need to establish journalism schools that can "make better journalists, who will make better newspapers, which will better serve the public" (1904, 46). Pulitzer meticulously describes what should be included in different courses, but he is surprisingly vague about what he believed was the most important part, namely, the journalistic principles. Throughout the essay, he refers to the importance of knowing about journalistic principles, for example, "principles ... must pervade all courses" (1904, 32), but nowhere does he specify what they should be. The place where he is most precise is in the final section of the essay, entitled "Public Service the Ultimate End" (1904, 46). To be "disinterested" – that is in Pulitzer's mind to be politically neutral – and to have the "intelligence" and "courage" to actively aid the public is about as concrete as he gets.

This imprecision when it comes to the principles of journalism is not only characteristic for Pulitzer and his contemporaries, as Chapter 2 about the precedents of constructive journalism showed. While the imprecision

DOI: 10.4324/9781003403098-3

could be considered neglect of the active journalists, editors, and owners of newspapers at the turn of the last century, it has been a necessity for later pioneers and proponents of the active journalism. Many proponents, promoters, and supporters of the later movements have kept their definitions open, fearing that overly specific principles might hinder or halt future experiments. This approach has had its benefits – it has excluded few from the outset, and it has fostered experiments in many newsrooms – but it has come at a price. The experiments that have followed have since resulted in doubts, confusion, and insecurity among opponents and supporters, and while the conceptual elasticity might have helped popularize the movements in their infancy, it has caused – in many ways – their downfall later on.

These years when a new movement is once again finding its way to newsrooms – and to classrooms at journalism schools, which Pulitzer championed – it is high time for more precise journalism principles of more active types of journalism. Otherwise, we risk that history repeats itself, and that practitioners and researchers alike once again fail to find out what – if anything – active journalism can contribute with. This chapter therefore starts by delineating the differences between past and present journalistic attempts to help society solve its problems. While the active approaches of the nineteenth, twentieth, and twenty-first centuries have many things in common, important journalistic principles set them apart from one another and from more traditional types of journalism. This chapter describes four different approaches to how journalists can be considered active in relation to the right-hand side of the journalistic compass, and it concludes with a discussion of how each of these four approaches relates to other principles in journalism, such as neutrality, objectivity, and responsibility.

Four approaches to active journalism

When analyzing what has been written – by proponents and opponents – about each of the three movements from the nineteenth, twentieth, and twenty-first centuries and relating this to what journalists, editors, and owners of news organizations have done journalistically in the name of these movements, four distinct but intertwined principles for how journalists can be considered active stand out. Each of these four principles relates to what journalism – and, by implication, journalists – is supposed to do in order to actively help societies solve their problems:

- Journalists should present problems.
- Journalists should present potentials.
- Journalists should promote solutions.
- Journalists should partake in solutions.

Principles of constructive journalism 43

Journalists should present problems

"[J]ournalism was shown to have a role in improving society by exposing the negative sides of life," Cathrine Gyldensted wrote on the opening pages of *From Mirrors to Movers* (2015, 6). She starts by pointing to some of journalism history's most famous journalists who have actively sought to move the world and explains that for years, she also worked in the belief that the best way to keep "society healthy" was to simply report on its problems, so that others could be alarmed and perhaps activated (2015, 9). Among the famous journalists she mentioned to was Jakob A. Riis, who believed that "fact is the mightiest lever" when it comes to prompting action among others who can help solve problems (Riis, 1901, 99). For years, Riis wrote about all kinds of social problems in New York City, and when this Danish immigrant at times found that his texts did not prompt action by others, he took pictures of the problems to make them – literally – visible to people.

Ulrik Haagerup makes the same point about what exposing societal problems can accomplish. He recounts how he was trained at journalism school to look for problems and how he went into the profession "to do good for society" (2017, 13). Haagerup turned out to be so good at finding problems as an investigative reporter that he even won the most prestigious journalistic prize in Denmark, the Cavling Prize, as one of the youngest journalists ever. Based on personal and historical examples, both pioneers of constructive here point to one of the ways in which journalists, editors, and owners of news organizations can actively attempt to help society solve its most pressing challenges, namely, by presenting problems and then leaving it to audiences – private citizens, authoritative decision-makers in political parties, companies, and others – to decide whether and what action is needed.

For many journalists, this principle – to present problems – has become so ingrained in the schooling and subsequent practice of journalism that they might not consider its historical circumstances and its ramifications. But Thomas Patterson has rightly noted that "the real bias of the press today is not that it is politically motivated," but rather that its bias has become "a preferred preference for the negative" (2002). At times, it seems that presenting problems has become an end rather than a means to other ends, such as solving societal problems. This was precisely the realization that both Haagerup and Gyldensted had: what they had worked for throughout their careers – "improving society" (Gyldensted, 2015, 6) and "to do good for society" (Haagerup, 2017, 13) – was not sufficiently accomplished when contended themselves with presenting problems. Both have also noted in their works how this approach can at times be even counterproductive and cause problems in itself for audiences.

This realization was one of the main reasons Haagerup and Gyldensted started searching for new and more productive approaches to journalism and arrived at constructive journalism. In this specific context, however, it is important to clarify that presenting problems can also be considered a deliberate and intentional attempt by some journalistic practitioners to actively help societies solve their problems. As such, journalists who present problems in their news stories can rightly claim to be constructive, since their work may occasionally help society solve its problems by alarming and convincing the public or its representatives to act. This helps explain why some journalistic practitioners and researchers have criticized the constructive journalism movement for conceptually monopolizing what they have worked for all along.

Journalists should present potentials

As Chapter 2 has shown, several generations of journalistic practitioners have found that presenting problems in order to improve society is problematic for several reasons, and that it should be supplemented, if not substituted, with presentation of potentials (what works already or could work in the future). The criticism of the problem-focused journalism was rather one-sided at the turn of the last century. Hearst, Pulitzer, and others primarily criticized what they occasionally termed "the old" journalism for not accomplishing enough. The later movements that developed in the twentieth and twenty-first centuries raised other points of criticism, and both the founders of the public journalism movement and the constructive journalism movement have argued that the negativity bias in much of traditional journalism distorts people's worldview and depresses audiences, which is bad enough in itself but may also cause them to avoid news altogether.

Critics have also argued that attempts to galvanize journalists and news organizations from criticism by always presenting something that is problematic to "somebody somewhere" rest on a flawed if not downright false premise. The point made is that presenting problems might be equally helpful for persons and organizations who want to take advantage of the mobilization potential of the news media. This criticism was first raised when public journalism developed and the criticism later resurfaced in the wake of the constructive journalism movement (see, e.g., Bro, 2012). No matter what the points of criticism focused on, the results have been a search for another approach to journalism, and in his column from 2008, where Haagerup first introduced the concept of "constructive news," he points to a different way in which journalists could be active in the future:

> There is also a need for solutions, inspiration and stories that the world is not only crazy, evil and dangerous. That it is also full of opportunities, joy, and quality of life.
>
> (Haagerup, 2008)

To present potentials constitutes a second approach to active journalism, and as noted in Chapters 1 and 2, there is a dual aspect to this approach. On the one hand, constructive journalism can relate to what is already working in society, for example, the things that go well and actually work, and, on the other hand, constructive journalism can relate to what might work in the future, for example, inspirations and solutions to what could work in the future. Taken together, these can be described as potentials (see Chapter 1), and as mentioned before, both aspects are evident in the first works by Haagerup and Gyldensted. In his 2008 column, Haagerup refers to a news story that might be inspirational for others, but he also points to a news program he was responsible for as news director in the Danish Broadcasting Corporation:

> After thousands of stories about stress, miserable bosses and problems with work-life balance, it was surely news when *Radioavisen* (the most listened to hourly radio news program in Denmark) informed us that a majority of Danes say they have a dream job.
>
> (Haagerup, 2008)

This particular news story pertains to something that already works.

News stories about things that work are described by Gyldensted as "positive journalism," and while this is a concept that Haagerup, in general, has stayed clear of in his publications, the concept is used repeatedly in Gyldensted's early works (2012, 2014 (with Bjerre); 2015). In Gyldensted's chapter in the first anthology edited by Haagerup (2012), she compares positive psychology with the field of journalism, and she notes that while much psychology focuses on personal problems, positive psychology emphasizes the "positive influences in a person's life," which are equally important to consider (2012, 191). Gyldensted's point is that while traditional journalism focuses on problems, we need a new, more "positive journalism" to understand that also good things happen in the world, and, she adds, that there is "good reason to revise our perception of the concept 'positive', which in journalism is almost synonymous with toothless, blue-eyed, and naïve" (2012, 192).

A few years later, Gyldensted defines "positive journalism" and "constructive journalism" as separate but connected approaches to journalism (2015, 13), and "constructive journalism" becomes an overall term used to describe what works already and what could work in the future. It is, as Karin McIntyre has noted, "a constructive news story does not require the inclusion of a solution" (2015, 16). Nonetheless, presenting such potentials as opposed to simply presenting problems is, in the words of Haagerup, an expression of "active" attempts to better aid, assist, and service the public, and when journalists present what goes well already, such news stories can be seen as an example of solutions already in place. In both instances, the presentation of potentials marks the second approach to active journalism, when one studies how journalists, editors, and news organizations, more generally, have worked to help society solve its problems over the cause of the nineteenth, twentieth, and twenty-first centuries.

Journalists should promote solutions

The two first approaches to active journalism differ when it comes to their focus. The first approach entails a focus on problems, and the second on potentials. But both approaches are based on the principle that it is ultimately up to people outside the newsrooms to decide what – if any – action should be taken in response to the problems or potentials presented. When it comes to the third way in which journalists can actively work to improve society, journalists will intentionally promote potentials that can help improve society, and here potentials take the form of solutions that point to possible, future actions. This marks an important difference, and here things become more complex for the founders of constructive journalism and the many later supporters of the movement. On one side, the founders have again and again underlined journalism's importance – in the past and in the present – in helping society solve its problem. On the other side, the founders are relative imprecise about just how active constructive journalists, editors, and owners of news organizations should be in this endeavor.

Haagerup and Gyldensted write repeatedly about the beneficial reciprocal relation between what happens inside and outside of newsrooms. "We should dare inspire solutions – and sometimes directly create the framework that can help the responsible do something about them," Haagerup writes (2012a, 236). A few years later, in the introduction to his first book in English, *Constructive Journalism* (2014, 4), he ponders: "How can we save journalism by helping it save the world." "Save the world," "help the world," "solve problems," and "make society better" are phrases used repeatedly by Haagerup and Gyldensted. One of the best examples is found in *From Mirrors to Movers* (2014), where Gyldensted uses the stick-and-carrot metaphor to highlight how journalists can move the world by presenting either problems or potentials. In both instances, readers are led to understand that the ultimate goal is to "move the world."

However, it seems that over the years, both founders, and in particular Haagerup, become increasingly clear about how far journalists should go to "save the world." In one of his later books, he draws up a list of what constructive journalism "is" and "is not" in his understanding of the concept. Under the list of what constructive journalism "is," he notes that journalists should be "tackling important issues facing society," be "forward-looking and future-oriented," and be "facilitating well-informed debate around solutions" (2017, 146). However, under the list of things "constructive journalism" "is not" and should not do, he specifically notes "proposing solutions to problems," "advocating one solution over another," and "activism in any shape or form" (2017, 146). Indeed, Haagerup repeatedly warns against "activism" in his later writings, which shows that there in his mind are limits to how far journalist should go in helping society solve its problems.

Gyldensted uses a similar wording and distinction. In a key passage in *From Mirrors to Movers* (2015), she writes that she hopes constructive journalists will "create content that involves and inspires readers, and to present journalism that adds perspective and gives people the opportunity to act" (2015, 7). She later sums up that constructive journalism "focusses on how ... problems can be solved," but this is not the same as taking responsibility for solving these problems. The two founders share the belief that journalists could – and indeed should – present potentials, including the sub-genre of solutions, but it is less clear if there are instances where journalist might do more than that. Matters are not made much clearer since both founders include examples of journalism in their books that go further than simply present solutions. In *From Mirrors to Movers* (2015), Gyldensted refers to inspiration from *The Guardian* in the UK, which campaigned actively for climate change. "The threat to our species is so severe that this is one of those rare subjects where you can move from reporting to campaigning. Just be transparent about it, explained the then editor-in-chief" (cf. Gyldensted, 2015, 154).

In *Constructive Journalism* (2014), Haagerup also refers to an editor-in-chief of a Danish regional newspaper, *Fyens Stiftstidende*, who actively promoted solution of several problems. In an interview with Haagerup, the editor-in-chief explains that

> we have asked ourselves if it is possible to supplement the traditional, critical observing role with a more activist approach, where the paper enters the arena to play a role and affect events. Our answer to that question is yes.
>
> (cf. Haagerup, 2014, 73)

The editor-in-chief points to several projects where they have taken what he calls an "activist approach," and while this approach goes well beyond what Haagerup believes is within the conceptual confines of constructive journalism, this editor-in-chief was actually named the first chairman of the board at Constructive Institute, Aarhus University, a few years later.

These different views on how far journalists should go to improve society will be discussed in more depth later. For now, it is important to note that the founders of the movement today promote a type of journalism that can be considered less active than the movements from the nineteenth and twentieth centuries. In the case of the public journalism movement, for example, several of the most well-known projects promoted solutions to problems. In the Pulitzer Prize-winning project, "A Question of Color", from 1994, the *Akron Beacon Journal* "tried to involve citizens in efforts to improve race relations"

(Haas, 2007, 84), and in another public journalism-project, "Taking Back Our Neighborhoods," from 1994, *The Charlotte Observer* actively attempted to mobilize its readers, viewers, and listeners to combat crime and violence in Charlotte. When the project was launched, the editor-in-chief wrote to readers that traditional "news coverage gets us nowhere" (Buckner cf. Charity, 1995), which was the reason why *The Charlotte Observer* would embark on a more active type of journalism that could help solve the local problems.[1]

When journalists partake in solutions

From presenting problems and presenting solutions to promoting solutions, journalists become more and more actively involved in helping societies solve their problems. The fourth way in which journalists can actively help societies solve their problems is by taking part themselves in the solutions. This approach falls outside of what the two founders of constructive journalism envision today, but as mentioned before the founders have in their early works pointed to such active types of journalism. One of the most debated examples (see, e.g., Jørgensen & Risbro, 2021) has been the regional Danish newspaper, *Fyens Stiftstidende*. This newspaper has experimented with many well-known constructive formats over the years, including systematic use of articles with graphic stamps like "This is how it can be solved," "How others do," and "3 good pieces of advice." The newspaper has also experimented with so-called "solution signals" so readers can quickly scan the pages of the newspaper and find constructive content.

However, this regional newspaper has embarked on projects that challenge how Haagerup and Gyldensted define constructive journalism. In 2014, Fyens Stiftstidende, for example, decided to advocate for the suspension of a bridge toll in order to help traffic in the region. The name of the project left little doubt about what the newspapers perceived to be the best solution: "Bridge Toll, No Thanks." This approach is in conflict with Haagerup's belief that journalists and news organizations should not propose solutions to problems and advocate one solution over another (2017, 146). Likewise, another project, "Three Lanes Now," left little doubt about what journalists and editors at the newspaper thought would be the best solution when it came to solving problems on the main motorway.[2]

While proponents, promoters, supporters, and practitioners of constructive journalism, in general, avoid this approach to active journalism, it has been integral part of the movements from the nineteenth and twentieth centuries. One of the supporters of the public journalism movement was Cole C. Campbell, editor of *St. Louis Post-Dispatch*. Campbell famously summed up a decade of experiments as follows: "We journalists have a great opportunity if we make problem solving the raison d'être of our news report" (1999, xv), and like many other journalists, editors, and owners of news organizations, his newspaper took active part in problem-solving. This active involvement was clear from the very names of the public journalism projects. The newspapers, radio, and television stations that were part of the movement often used pronouns in their project titles, like "we," "us," and "ourselves," and thus included themselves, linguistically and literately, in the problem-solving process. Participation in problem-solving took many different forms. They organized forums, facilitated public debates, and used their reporting resources to describe how individuals, organizations, and others had worked to solve problems, and at times journalists and editors became very active problem solvers.

A good example of the latter was a special public journalism project in which *Los Angeles Times* for many months focused on how to improve literacy among children in Southern California. As part of this project, several journalists and editors volunteered to help at local schools and as such not only worked to prompt others to act but contributed personally to the solution. Such active involvement was heavily criticized by other people in the news industry, but the proponents of public journalism argued that it was possible to maintain neutrality while engaging in problem-solving. One of the founders, Jay Rosen, argued that the guiding principle for public journalism was "proactive neutrality" where journalism is "neutral" because it "prescribes no chosen solution and favors no particular party of interest," but it is also "proactive in its belief that journalism can in certain cases intervene in the service of broad public values without compromising its integrity" (1996, 13). Another founder, Davis Merritt, wrote that journalists could – and indeed should – be what he called "fair-minded participants" who are "neutral on specifics" but "move far enough beyond detachment to care about whether resolution occurs" (1995, 116).

Arguments for this type of active journalism took a less subtle form a hundred years prior to public journalism, when William Randolph Hearst, Joseph Pulitzer, and others promoted their work. "(H)as it a right to protect the public interest by deeds as well as words," asked William Randolph Hearst rhetorically with reference to his newspaper. The answer was not surprising: "*The Journal* holds the theory that a newspaper may fitly render any public service within its power," Hearst proclaimed and promised that *The Journal* would be "ready to act when public interest require action, and to act in the way to accomplish results." That was a promise Hearst kept – to act by deeds as well as words – and in the case of the Cisneros affair, *The Journal* orchestrated, carried out a prison break in a foreign country and later boasted about the accomplishment on its front page and by way of a parade at Times Square in New York City. There were other examples where *The Journal* took matters in its own hands,[3] and when Hearst did not boast about the accomplishments, he did not refrain from criticizing others.

"May a newspaper properly do things or are its legitimate functions confined to talking about them? That is the chief question at issue between the representatives of the new and the old journalism," *The Journal* wrote on one occasion and criticized newspapers that "contented themselves ... with pointing out existing evils or giving warning of impending dangers." *The Journal* also wrote with reference to its many competitors like *The New York Times*: "They gave the alarm and whether it was heeded or not was no concerns of theirs." While Hearst's *The Journal* was certainly a leading example of "journalism that does things," the newspaper and its editor-in-chief were not alone. Pulitzer's *The World* also embarked on a number of projects, and both newspapers took it upon themselves to help solve all sorts of problems. *The World* helped the poor in New York by preparing thousands of dinners for Thanksgiving and Christmas and helped establish schools, and *The Journal* set up soup kitchens in the winter. Other newspapers took it upon themselves to, in Hearst's words, "fitly render any public service within its power," among them *The New York Tribune*, which offered summer outings for poor children in New York.[4]

Different degrees of active journalism

Time to sum up. The history of journalism suggests that journalists who actively want to help society solve its problems can do so in four ways: (1) by presenting problems and leaving it to others to decide what to do, if anything, about the problems; (2) by presenting potentials and leaving it to others to decide what to do, if anything, about them; (3) by promoting solutions and attempting to prompt action among others; and finally (4) by participating in solutions themselves. Studying the major movements in the nineteenth, twentieth, and twenty-first centuries shows that each collective endeavor has worked to do more than simply present problems (active journalism in the first degree), but there are differences between the movements, when it comes to how active the founders believed journalists – and by implication the news media – should be. Here, the founders of the constructive journalism movement seem to be the least active since they have come to believe that constructive journalism should only "move" – to paraphrase Gyldensted (1995) – the world by presenting problems and potentials.

A closer look at what journalists, editors, and owners of news organizations have done in the name of "constructive journalism" has revealed examples of journalistic projects that have clearly overstepped the constraints now dictated by the founders. But since the founders have been careful – especially in the early years, not to hinder or halt experiments by being too precise about what constructive journalism is and is not – the initiators of these projects have on several occasions termed their own work "constructive." Such conceptual difficulties also plagued the public journalism movement that developed in the late twentieth century. While one of the founders, Jay Rosen, has at times downplayed just how active public journalists should be in "problem-solving," other proponents, promoters, and supporters of public journalism have pursued a more active approach in words as well as deeds. Believing that the news media stood in the way of society solving its problems, many journalists, editors, and owners of news organizations have actively promoted and at times even taken part in problem-solving.

However, the oldest of the three movements – "the journalism that does things," as Hearst at times dubbed it – exemplifies the most active approach of the three movements. One of the most insightful chroniclers of this era, W. Joseph Campbell, has described this journalism as "restless" (2006, 87), always on the lookout for new problems to solve and new things to set in motion to move the world in what was perceived as a better direction. Campbell has even noted that the "restless" journalism at times also became downright "reckless" (2006, 87), in particular how it was practiced by William Randolph Hearst, his editors and journalists at *The World*. Hearst, Pulitzer, Lord Northcliffe, and other proponents and supporters of the active journalism around the turn of the last century could at times have difficulties distinguishing between their own interests and that of the "disinterested" newspapers they heralded at other times. This led to frequent accusations that these newspaper owners violated the neutrality and impartiality that they themselves have helped instigate and propagate in the first place.

The different degrees of active journalism illustrate that it is not sufficient to differentiate between a passive and an active journalism, when we want to describe differences and similarities between traditional journalism and the active movements from the nineteenth, twentieth, and twenty-first centuries. Instead, this dichotomy in the journalistic compass can be seen as a continuum (see Figure 3.1),[5] where active journalism can build on four different approaches. The least active of the four is the presentation of problems, where journalists intentionally publish news stories to alarm their audiences, but where the responsibility for, what to do about the problems, is left to readers, listeners, and others. This can be considered active journalism in the first degree. Active journalism in the second degree is when journalists intentionally present potentials. Here, journalists feel responsible for presenting audiences with news stories about what works already or could work in the future, but what these news stories ultimately amount to in terms of solving problems in society is the responsibility of audiences, not of reporters, editors, and owners of news organizations.

In active journalism of the third degree, journalists do not leave it to people outside the newsroom to decide what to do about problems or potentials. Here, active journalists are dedicated to ensuring positive change, and they do so by promoting solutions that other people can use to solve societal problems. These active journalists feel a responsibility for solving societal problems, but it is only in the fourth degree that active journalists also themselves partake in the actual solutions and do not simply leave the solutions to others outside the newsroom. The third and fourth degrees might, to some observers, constitute activism in the sense that journalists here work intentionally to bring about

Principles of constructive journalism

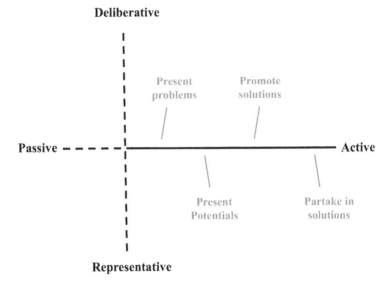

Figure 3.1 The active journalism continuum.

change, and that they also take on a social responsibility for this. But it is important not to confuse activism with advocacy, where the latter refers those who work on behalf of a particular organization or person (such as political parties and political candidates) to promote their viewpoints. Such advocacy journalism was something that Hearst, Pulitzer, and at times also Northcliffe (Chalaby, 2000) at times were accused of practicing.

While the continuum of active approaches makes it clear that there is much that differs between these four degrees of active journalism and between the three movements from the last century and a half, it is also important to note some of the pivotal similarities between the three. Michael Schudson has, in this context, made an important point about the public journalism movement that is also relevant when looking at the other movements. Writing at the height of success for the public journalism movement, Schudson noted that despite all of the controversies public journalism had caused among journalistic practitioners and researchers, it was still essentially just a "version of the very same ideology that dominates the world of professional journalists" (1999, 121). Schudson's point was that the authority of the news (e.g., where to find news, what to select, whom to include, and how to present news stories) was still nested with journalists, and he therefore described public journalism as a "conservative" reform movement (1999, 122).

In light of that, the constructive journalism movement might be described as an even more conservative reform movement in journalism. For all of their criticism of more traditional types of journalism, the founders of constructive journalism have consistently underlined that this new type of journalism should not replace the old one. It is a question of supplementing rather than substituting, they have written, and the journalism the founders advocate for today is by all accounts less active than that of their predecessors in previous centuries. Not surprisingly, the least conservative of the three movements is the active journalism from the late nineteenth century. *The Journal* publicly explained that it had a "*duty* to take prominent and participatory roles in public life, to act when no other agency was able or willing" (cf. Campbell, 2006, 87), and it criticized other newspapers and the authorities for not being as successful in helping public life.

"But for the Journal, the arm of the law would have been palsied," *The Journal* wrote after it had solved the so-called "East River murder mystery" by identifying a victim and leading the police to the chief suspect. "To bring a murderer to justice is to discharge a great public duty," *The Journal* noted. It also boasted about the Cisnero affair, calling it the "greatest journalistic coup of this age." Despite the active newspapers' indisputable commercial success, the active journalism of the nineteenth century certainly had its critics within the ranks of journalism, and no one was perhaps more vocal than Alfred Ochs of *The New York Times*.[6] Ochs's newspaper had a more restrained and detached approach to things. When it came to the East River murder mystery, *The Times* was alarmed and appalled by the way *The Journal* had injected itself in the case, and even more so with the Cisnero affair, where it had orchestrated a prison break. *The Times* wrote that it feared such activities could halt international diplomacy or even start a war.

The essence of the heated debates between the newspapers at the turn of the last century – at times conducted on the front pages – had to do with journalistic principles such as objectivity, neutrality, and responsibility. Such debates over the principles of journalism have also surfaced when public journalism and later constructive journalism gained popularity. When it came to public journalism, the two founders attempted to explain, in each their way, that it was indeed possible to be active and take greater responsibility for the world without compromising objectivity, neutrality, and impartiality. But not all contemporary journalistic practitioners and researchers believed in Rosen's and Merritt's claims relating to the notions of "proactive neutrality" (Rosen, 1996, 13) and "fair-minded participants" (Merritt, 1995, 116). In a column in *The New York Times*, a former editor-in-chief described public journalism as "Fix-It Journalism" (Frankel, 1995), and that was not meant as praise.

"American journalism sorely needs improvement. But redefining journalism as a quest for a better tomorrow will never compensate for its poor performance at explaining yesterday," the former editor-in-chief wrote, and he ended the column by stating, "Journalists should leave reform to reformers" (Frankel, 1995). There were many other negative comments about public journalism and also much name-calling. This had also been the case a hundred years earlier, where *The Times* referred to the competitors at *The World* and *The Journal* as "our esteemed freak contemporaries" in several editorials, and where the derogatory term "yellow journalism" was also introduced.[7] In *The Washington Post*, the editor-in-chief referred to the newspaper's policy on standards and ethics, according to which editors and reporters should "avoid active involvement in any partisan causes – politics, community affairs, social action, demonstrations – that could compromise or seem to compromise our ability to report and edit fairly." The editor-in-chief explained that he no longer exercised the right to vote and privately refused to take sides in political disputes, since it would make him too involved in society.

Another critic from the industry accused promoters and practitioners of public journalism of having misunderstood what journalism is all about:

> Newspapers are supposed to explain the community, not convene it. News reporters are supposed to explore the issues, not solve them. Newspapers are supposed to expose the wrongs, not campaign against them.
> (cf. Carey, 1999, 50)

These were points of criticism that echoed what the active journalists in the late nineteenth century encountered. Back then, *The Times* noted that readers should have news presented "with entire impartiality," and it is no coincidence that one of journalism's most recited slogans, "All the News That's Fit to Print," was introduced on its front page in this period. It was a way of differentiating *The Times* from Hearst's and Pulitzer's newspapers, which were, in every sense of the word, all over the world, and as the more passive journalism – "counter-activist" in the words of W. Joseph Campbell (2006, 6) – gained popularity in the twentieth century Ochs was heralded for having introduced a new principle in daily journalism that meant printing all the important news regardless of what the paper felt about its implication.

The same debates have ensued with the rise of the constructive journalism movement, and both founders have referred to this criticism, although with different approaches to the criticism. In one of her books, Gyldensted and her co-author Malene Bjerre present what they describe as "myths" about constructive journalism that they have often encountered.[8] The fourth myth states that "constructive journalism is not objective," to which Gyldensted and Bjerre reply: "Correct. But no journalism is objective. Objectivity can be defined as presenting and communicating everything about a given case. Journalism is slices of larger reality" (2014, 27). Their point is that the concept of objectivity is basically "faulty," since journalism will always entail a framing where some things are chosen and other things are discarded, and in several of Gyldensted's other works, she refers to journalists, editors, and others who have approached the issue of objectivity and neutrality in different ways. One editor who has experimented with constructive journalism has noted that "(o)bjectivity is an illusion. All reporting is a product of subjective choices made by the people producing the stories" (cf. Gyldensted, 2014, 35).

Haagerup has another take on objectivity. In several of his books, he refers to pivotal issues relating to constructive journalism that, according to Haagerup, might lead to discussions with oneself, colleagues, editors, and people inside and outside the media (see, e.g., Haagerup, 2014, 111). One of these issues relates directly to objectivity, impartiality, and responsibility, and here Haagerup writes:

> Do not cross the line of subjectivity. Constructive news argues that a good story can be inspirational, and that journalism can facilitate a better public debate on possible solutions to the problems facing society. But it is not the job of any professional journalist to define what the right solutions are.
> (2017, 141)

His point, in other words, is that constructive journalism can indeed be considered objective, and it is not until it becomes "activist in any shape or form" (Haagerup, 2017, 146) that it becomes subjective. All of which is a reminder that all of the historical attempts to do more than simply present problems have always sparked debates over objectivity, neutrality, and the responsibility of journalists and journalism.

Different approaches to objectivity in active journalism

In order to understand the conflicting statements by the founders of constructive journalism, and to more fully grasp why the issue of objectivity, neutrality and responsibility always comes to be discussed in relation to active journalism, it can be helpful to look to research. From the time the concept of objectivity became an object of scholarly study, scores of researchers have sought to clarify its various components and uncover its different meanings and importance in different journalistic contexts (see, e.g., Schudson, 2001; Tuchman, 1972; Westerståhl, 1983). Three components are of particular importance for journalism, generally, and for constructive journalism, especially, and they relate to an important distinction Stephen Ward makes in his seminal book *The Invention of Journalism Ethics: The Path to Objectivity and Beyond* (2004). Ward operates with, what he refers to as three "senses" of objectivity: "Ontological (external objects, facts), epistemic or epistemological (beliefs and attitudes), and procedurals (decisions)" (2004, 16). Ward describes journalistic objectivity as a hybrid of these three senses:

> Ontological objectivity in journalism involves telling it "the way it is." Reports are epistemically objective if they adhere to good reporting

methods and standards. Reports are procedurally objective if they present information in a manner that is fair to sources and to rival viewpoints

(2004, 19)

In the words of Ward, the first sense stresses the importance of "facts," the second "procedures," and the third "impartiality," and what is important here is the fact that between the two of them, Haagerup and Gyldensted touch upon all three senses.

The first sense of objectivity relates to factual descriptions in journalism. Ontology comes from the Greek words *on* ("being") and *logia* ("study"), and news stories are ontologically objective if they contain accurate descriptions of the world.[9] Many journalists, editors, and owners of news organizations contend that they are objective, since news reports – in general – contain accurate descriptions of events, issues, statements, and what else makes the news. However, the founders and many later supporters of constructive journalism reject that claim, and they do so on the grounds that traditional journalism is preoccupied with problems and therefore leaves out the potentials of what happens in the world, that is, things that go well or could go well in the future. Here, Gyldensted and Haagerup are essentially basing their critique on the ontological sense of objectivity, and since the very first introduction of the concept of constructive news, this point has been the primary basis of their criticism of traditional journalism.

In Haagerup's column from 2008, Haagerup asks rhetorically, "Are we giving a fair picture of the world? Or do our habits, our world view and our journalistic tradition help to paint a picture that becomes a bit skewed?" Haagerup also asks, "Is our glass always half empty instead of half full?" and "Are we so focused on talking about the holes in the cheese that we sometimes forget to talk about the cheese?" (2008). In all three instances, his point is that journalism with a problem-focus by design leaves out much of what takes place in the world. Gyldensted makes the same point. As mentioned previously, she introduces dichotomies, like "male" and "female," "hot" and cold," and "summer" and "winter," and she explains that we also need "negative" and "constructive" news stories, since it takes them both to "portray the world accurately," as she described it (2015, 8).

Both founders believe that if journalists were to add a constructive perspective in their news stories, it would essentially enable them to see "the world with both eyes" and thereby present the "best obtainable version of the truth" (Haagerup, 2014). For Haagerup, such an approach amounts to being "objective," as he concludes it in *Constructive News* (2017). While Gyldensted concurs with the importance of wider perspective, she has another take on what it means to be objective, and this explains why she refers to constructive journalism as being "subjective" (2014, 27). In *Textbook in Constructive Journalism*, which she co-wrote with Malene Bjerre, the authors suggest that all journalism is essentially subjective. Their point is that journalism entails framing – "from idea to research to presentation" of a news story, since journalists select and make some things more salient while they also reject and tone down others, and here the two authors essentially point to another sense of objectivity that relates to epistemology.

Epistemology comes from the Greek words *episteme* ("understanding" or "knowledge") and *logos* ("reason" or "argument"), and while objectivity in the ontological sense of the word relates to what the world is like (the facts), the epistemological sense of objectivity refers to the process in which journalists come to know what the world is like.[10] Gyldensted and Bjerre stress that no form or type of journalism can be "objective" due to the inevitable subjective choices made in the work process. However, they clearly stipulate that regardless of how they and others might define "objectivity," all journalistic practitioners should exercise and exhibit fairness, balance, and honesty in their work process (Gyldensted & Bjerre, 2014, 27). The statement shows that part of the disagreement between the two founders of constructive has to do with different understandings of the meaning of objectivity, and that they essentially refer to what Ward would describe as different "senses" of objectivity. But there is even a third sense at play here, and it comes to mind when Haagerup warns that constructive journalism should present news stories about what works or could work in the future, but they should not be activists.

The third sense of journalistic objectivity is in some ways more complex and is comprised of several components and categories, but in this context, it is of particular importance that this third sense relates to "impartiality," "neutrality," and "detachment" (Ward, 2004, 19). As noted above, the founders of constructive journalism are, in general, more restrained and conservative that their predecessors from the nineteenth and twentieth centuries, when it comes to how active journalists should be and when it comes to improving society. While the active journalists, editors, and owners of news organizations at the turn of the last century had few hesitations in terms of what they might do to promote action among others or even partake in what they believed were good solutions to societal problems, the public journalists of the late twentieth century were more hesitant. Even so it was an important constitutive element of public journalism that journalism should worry less about and more about "Getting the connections rights," as the title of one of Jay Rosen's books stated (1996), and ensuring "Community-connectedness" as another title read (Rosen, 1993).

The founders of public journalism came to discuss many of the same issues as the founders of the constructive journalism debates today, and in some respects, the works of Jay Rosen and Davis Merritt seem more thought through, when it comes to the roles and responsibilities of journalists. Rosen and Merritt believed that it was in accordance with time-honored journalistic principles for practitioners of the craft to be what they termed "proactive" (Rosen, 1996, 13) and "participants" in public affairs (Merritt, 1995, 116), as long as journalists were "neutral" and prescribed "no chosen solution and

58 *Principles of constructive journalism*

favors no particular party of interest" (Rosen, 1996, 13) and "fair" and "neutral on specifics" (Merritt, 1995, 116) when it came to what the right solutions might be.[11] In this sense, the founders of public journalism had more in common with the active journalism at the turn of the last century, since people like Merritt believed that it was in accordance with journalistic principles to "move far enough beyond detachment to care about whether resolution occurs" (1995, 116).

Studying the history of journalism through the prism of the principle of objectivity, several similarities and differences between passive and active types of journalism become clearer, and paying attention to different senses of objectivity might also be helpful for practitioners of the constructive journalism movement in the future. The different senses help explain, at least in part, why even the founders of the movement at times have seemed at odds, and in many of the discussions that accompany constructive journalism as it is spreading in newsrooms and classrooms around the world, it also seems as if supporters and opponents are both relating and referring to different aspects of objectivity. In this way, constructive journalism becomes a catalyst – a critical incident – that challenges us to think deeply about the different senses of objectivity, how they relate, and under what circumstances. These are issues that will also be addressed in Chapter 4, where the ways in which journalistic principles are operationalized into concrete practices are at the center.

Notes

1 A much debated U.S. poll – and often referenced by supporters of public journalism – from the 1990s showed that 71 percent of U.S. citizens contend that the "media stand in the way of making America solving its problems" (cf. Zelizer, 1999, 154)
2 The same has been noted by two former fellows at the Constructive Institute. In their book *Constructive Journalism: From Idea to Story* (2021), they write about the difference between activism and constructive journalism. "In our view, journalism crosses the line from constructive journalism to activism when a media such as Fyens Stiftstidende chooses to take an active position on whether or not there should be a charge for driving across the Storebælt," they write with reference to one of this regional newspaper's projects (Jørgensen & Risbro, 2021, 184).
3 The Cisnero affair was not the only time where Hearst was accused of starting a war with other nations. When the illustrator Frederick Remington, complained to Hearst about being sent to Cuba to cover a possible insurrection, who was apparently nowhere in sight, Hearst famously replied by telegram: "You furnish the pictures, I'll furnish the war." Historians still debate if Hearst really intended to instigate war.
4 On several occasions, Hearst described "the journalism of action" as a theory and a "model of journalism." Regardless of the label, this approach was in the words of one of the period's chroniclers, Joseph Campbell, defined by a "panoply of strategies through which Hearst's Journal would inject itself as a participant" (2006, 19). It often seemed that there was literally nothing that *The Journal* and its bigger competitor *The World* would not do to provide what they considered a public service. Hearst's belief that "when things are going wrong," a newspaper "should set them right, if possible," is perhaps the guiding principle he is best remembered for. It is important to note, however, that Hearst, Pulitzer, and others who took part

Principles of constructive journalism 59

in solving problems also worked to prompt the other principles mentioned in this chapter. At times, *The World* and *The Journal* limited themselves to presenting problems; at times, they presented solutions; and at times, they promoted solutions.

5 A few other researchers have touched upon this issue and introduced different types of continuums. One example is Caroline Fishers so-called "advocacy continuum" (2016). Fisher's continuum highlights that journalists, intentionally or unintentionally, can include elements of advocacy in their news work, whereby they can come to argue "in support of an idea, event or a person" (2016, 712). Another example is the work by Thomas Hanitzsch. Hanitzsch has suggested that journalistic intervention – for example, when it comes to covering politics and politicians – can be seen as a continuum. "The intervention pole of the continuum becomes manifest in role models like the 'participant', 'advocate', and 'missionary' with journalists taking more active role in their reporting" (2007, 373). This work, in part, resembles that of other researchers who have attempted to model different journalistic role conceptions (see, e.g., Donsbach & Patterson, 2004).

6 It is worth mentioning that W. Joseph Campbell also points to a "third paradigm" that was present at the turn of the last century. The first paradigm is the "journalism of action" represented by *The World* and *The Journal*; the second is the detached, counteractivist paradigm represented by *The New York Times*; and the third is the literary approach pursued by contemporaries like Lincoln Steffens. In the words of Campbell, "Steffens shunned veteran newspapermen and instead recruited college-educated writers who had little or no experience in journalism. He then sent them out to write, to hone their talent by telling stories about the joys, hardship, and serendipity of life in New York City" (2006, 6).

7 While Alfred Ochs of *The Times* did not invent the name "yellow press" – it was first used by *The New York Press* – it soon caught on in Ochs's and other newspapers at the time. With explicit reference to "active" journalism, *The Times* noted that readers should have news presented "with entire impartiality," and it is no coincidence that one of journalism's most recited slogans, "All the News That's Fit to Print," was introduced on its front page in this period. It was a way of differentiating *The Times* from Hearst's and Pulitzer's newspapers, which were, in every sense of the word, all over the world. Although it was believed at the time that active journalism would be the more successful approach – at one point, *The World* even described reporters and editors at *The Times* as "derelicts of journalism" – things turned out differently. Ochs was later heralded by a fellow newspaper owner for having introduced "a new principle in daily journalism ... of printing all the important news regardless of what the paper felt about its implication."

8 Cathrine Gyldensted and Malene Bjerre point to four myths about constructive journalism: Myth 1: "Constructive journalism is uncritical," Myth 2: "Constructive journalism puts a lid on conflicts," Myth 3: "Constructive journalism is not hard news," and Myth 4: "Constructive journalism is not objective" (2014, 46–49).

9 In *The Invention of Journalism Ethics* (2004), Stephen Ward notes that in the medieval era, objectivity and subjectivity meant the opposite of what we mean by these terms today. The English noun "objectivity" goes back to the classical Latin verb *obicere* – "to oppose" and "to place a hinderance before." By medieval times, the Latin noun *objectum* referred to "a visible object placed before someone" (Ward, 2004, 15).

10 This echoes another description of objectivity as a "defensible, rigorous, and transparent" (Kovach & Rosenstiel, 2014, 11) process rather than claiming that journalists can cover all events in the world precisely.

11 Based on his study of the public journalism movement, Tanni Haas has noted that "the distinctions between problem-reporting and problem-solving, and between political neutrality and political advocacy, are untenable in a very fundamental sense" (Haas, 2007, 77).

References

Bro, Peter (2012) "Historien om den nyttige nyhedsformidling" ["The History of Usefull News Reporting"]. In *En konstruktiv Nyhed* [A Constructive News Story], edited by Ulrik Haagerup, 129–143, Århus: Ajour.

Campbell, Cole C. (1999) "Foreword: Journalism as a democratic act." In *The Idea of Public Journalism*, edited by Theodore L. Glasser, xiii–xxix, New York: Guildford Press.

Campbell, W. Joseph (2006) *The Year That Defined American Journalism: 1897 and the Clash of Paradigms*. New York: Routledge.

Carey, James, W. (1999) "In defense of public journalism." In *The Idea of Public Journalism*, edited by Theodore Glasser, 49–66, New York: Guildford Press.

Chalaby, Jean K. (2000) "Northcliffe's journalism." *Media History* 6 (1): 33–44.

Charity, Arthur (1995) *Doing Public Journalism*. New York: Guildford Press.

Donsbach, Wolfgang and Thomas E. Patterson (2004) "Political news journalists: Partisanship, professionalism, and political roles in five countries." In *Comparing Political Communication: Theories, Cases, and Challenges*, edited by Frank Esser and Barbara Pfetsch, 251–270, New York: Cambridge University Press.

Fisher, Caroline (2016) "The advocacy continuum: Towards a theory of advocacy in journalism." *Journalism* 17 (6): 711–726.

Frankel, Max (1995) "Fix-It Journalism." *New York Times Magazine*, May 21.

Gyldensted, Cathrine (2012) "Spøgelset fra watergate – Nixon ud af nyhederne" [The ghost from Watergate – Nixon out of the news]. In *En Konstruktiv Nyhed* [A Constructive News Story], edited by Ulrik Haagerup, 185–198, Århus: Ajour.

Gyldensted, Cathrine (2015) *From Mirrors to Movers: Five Elements of Positive Psychology in Constructive Journalism*. Charleston, SC: Group Publishing.

Gyldensted, Cathrine and Malene Bjerre (2014) *Håndbog i Konstruktiv Journalistic* [Handbook in Constructive Journalism]. Århus: Ajour.Haagerup, Ulrik (2008) "Konstruktive nyheder" [Constructive News]. *Politiken*, December 6.

Haagerup, Ulrik (2012a) "Vejen frem" [The Road Ahead]. In *En konstruktiv Nyhed* [A Constructive News Story], edited by Ulrik Haagerup, 217–236, Århus: Ajour.

Haagerup, Ulrik (2014) *Constructive News: How to Save the Media and Democracy with Journalism of Tomorrow*. New York: InnoVatio Publishing.

Haagerup, Ulrik (2017) *Constructive News: How to Save the Media and Democracy with Journalism of Tomorrow*. Aarhus, Denmark: Aarhus University Press.

Haas, Tanni (2007) *The Pursuit of Public Journalism: Theory, Practice, and Criticism*. New York: Routledge.

Hanitzsch, Thomas (2007) "Deconstructing journalism culture: Towards an universal theory". *Communication Theory* 17 (4): 367–385.

Jørgensen, Kristina Lund and Jakob Risbro (2021) *Konstruktiv Journalistik: Fra Ide til Historie* [Constructive Journalism: From Idea to Story]. Århus: Forlaget Ajour.

Kovach, Bill and Tom Rosenstiel (2014/2001) *The Elements of Journalism: What News People Should Know and the Public Should Expect*. New York: Three Rivers Press.

McIntyre, Karen (2015) *Constructive Journalism: The Effects of Positive Emotions and Solution Information in News Stories*. Doctoral Dissertation, University of North Carolina, Chapel Hill, NC.

Merritt, Davis (1995) *Public Journalism and Public Life*. Mahwah, NJ: Lawrence Erlbaum Associates.

Patterson, Thomas (2002) *The Vanishing Voter: Public Involvement in an Age of Uncertainty*. New York: Knopf.
Pulitzer, Joseph (1904) *The School of Journalism at Columbia University*. New York: Columbia University Press.
Rosen, Jay (1993) *Community-Connectedness: Passwords for Public Journalism*. St. Petersburg: Poynter Institute for Media Studies.
Rosen, Jay (1996) *Getting the Connections Right*. New York: The Twentieth Century Fund Press.
Schudson, Michael (1999) "What public journalism knows about journalism but doesn't know about 'public'." In *The Idea of Public Journalism*, edited by Theodore Glasser, 118–133. New York: Guildford Press.
Schudson, Michael (2001) "The objectivity norm in American journalism." *Journalism* 2 (2): 149–171.
Tuchman, Gaye (1972) "Objectivity as strategic ritual: An Examination of newsmen's notions of objectivity." *American Journal of Sociology* 77 (4): 660–679.
Ward, Stephen J. A. (2004) *The Invention of Journalism Ethics: The Path to Objectivity and Beyond*. Montreal: McGill-Queen's University Press.
Westerståhl, Jörgen (1983) "Objective news reporting." *Communication Research* 10 (3): 403–424.
Zelizer, Barbie (1999) "Making the neighborhood work: The improbabilities of public journalism." In *The Idea of Public Journalism*, edited by Theodore Glasser, 152–172, New York: Guildford Press.

4 Practices of constructive journalism

Many of the first journalists, editors, and owners of newspapers who believed that journalism should do more than simply present problems were highly successful on a personal level. Some of them became wealthy, some of them made names for themselves, and some of them did both those things and more. But when it came to ensuring the active journalism, they praised and practiced for posterity, they failed, by most accounts, and throughout the twentieth century, the presentation of societal problems has become the gold standard of journalism. The bigger the problems, the better and the biggest of them all are awarded front pages and win prizes. Some of the reasons why the "journalism that does things" did not live on are obvious. There were few, if any institutions, organizations, associations, conferences, seminars, and publications and other platforms and venues around the turn of the last century that could function as a fixture for the principles and practice of active journalism. They were, quite simply, difficult to pass on. Other reasons had to do with the "panoply of strategies" (Campbell, 2006, 19) and the constant experiments with new methods and modes of presentation, which blurred things when it came to what these iconic figures in journalism had worked for.

Things were different a hundred years later when a new generation of journalists once again attempted to prompt and promote a type of journalism that does more than present problems – this time joined by journalistic lecturers and researchers at universities and journalism schools. Now, journalists were trained in classrooms rather than in newsrooms, scores of textbooks about journalism had been published, and numerous professional associations were established (locally, nationally, and internationally) along with associations for more specific approaches, such as investigative reporting, political journalism, sports journalism, digital journalism, and obituary writing. Add to that the proliferation of seminars and conferences held at regular intervals and a large number of journalistic prizes, that had been established, following Pulitzer's example, to inspire and influence practitioners of the craft. Indeed, it has been argued that few professions, if any, have as many prizes as journalism, and in academia, it is noted that when scholars meet at conferences, they do so to criticize each other, but when journalists meet, they give out prizes to one another.

DOI: 10.4324/9781003403098-4

All these places where present and future generations of journalist can meet each other and be inspired by others have surely contributed to the speed with which the news of the movement of the twentieth century spread around the world. The public journalism movement – also known under other names, such as civic journalism and community journalism – thereby became a catalyst for widespread discussions about the role and responsibilities of journalism. However, while the interest for experimenting with the new journalistic principles spread, journalistic practitioners and researchers started to wonder how these principles could be operationalized into concrete practices. Here, there were little help. Around the ten-year mark of the movement, Barbie Zelizer complained that the "mechanics" of public journalism had not been made sufficiently clear. "[T]he prescriptive domain of public journalism is almost non-existent. Despite the fact that there are numerous publications about public journalism, no manual or checklist stipulates how one is supposed to engage in it," she wrote and added that if public journalism was "to stay more than an idea, it needs to have time and space to ground itself into practice" (1999, 157).

That never happened, the movement lost popularity, scholarly publications about public journalism are now written in past tense, and few practitioners refer to it in newsrooms. As such, history is a reminder of the importance of clarifying both principles and the accompanying practices. The same problems were evident when constructive journalism was launched in the beginning of the twenty-first century and soon gained ground in news organizations around the world. At first, constructive journalism seemed to be mostly characterized by what it was not and what it could become later, but as more and more journalists and editors attempted to operationalize the principles of constructive journalism into practice, the differences and similarities with problem-based journalism are becoming increasingly clear. This chapter describes and discusses how the practice of constructive journalism has developed, and it focuses especially on what constructive journalism has become, how it is presented to audiences, and who is invited to take part in news stories.[1]

Approaches to constructive journalism

When constructive journalism was launched, it was based on what in hindsight seems like a modest ambition. "We must dare to supplement our traditional news criteria with a new one: constructive news," wrote Ulrik Haagerup in 2008. The heading of the column in the Danish newspaper where the new movement was launched simply read "Constructive News," and the subheading "Good news does not have to be death, destruction, and misery – it can also be inspiration and news solutions" (Haagerup, 2008). Perhaps not surprising at this early stage of what was later to become a worldwide movement, the column mentioned almost no concrete examples of the new type of journalism, Haagerup called for. Instead, the column primarily focused on what constructive journalism was not, what constructive journalism could – perhaps – become in the future, and most importantly what contemporary problems in the news media constructive news could be considered an answer to.

The column contained many examples of more traditional types of news, where more or less pressing societal problems were presented in well-known formats with "villains, victims, drama, and conflicts," as Haagerup summarized, what he described as the classic approach. The closest he came to presenting concrete examples of "constructive news" were two recent news stories and a news story that had been dropped. Both recent news stories had been produced by reporters at the Danish Broadcasting Corporation, where Haagerup was news director at the time, and the first news story presented a new poll showing a majority of Danes believed they held their "dream job." The second news story described how a Danish hospital had solved problems with overworked nurses. However, Haagerup devoted most lines in the column to the story that could have been, namely, a recent report about unemployment rates among immigrant women in Danish municipalities. The rates were high everywhere, except in one municipality where the report read "0 percent."

A reporter from the Danish Broadcasting Company who was thinking about doing a story about the unemployment rates decided to find out if there was a problem with the report. He contacted the municipality with 0 percent unemployment, which confirmed the result and told him about a consultant – by the name Lene – who connected local immigrant women and local companies in novel ways. According to Haagerup, the reporter discussed this explanation with an editor, and following this discussion, the journalist and editor decided not to go with the story about "the Lene effect" because they did not see a conflict in the story. Haagerup has used the story about the Lene effect repeatedly in his later books (see, e.g., 2012a, 2014), because it effectively illustrates two distinctly different approaches to journalism: one that focuses on problems, and another approach that focuses on what have been termed "potentials" in the previous chapters. Haagerup described such potentials in his column like this:

> Solutions, inspiration, and stories that the world is not only crazy, evil, and dangerous. That it is also full of opportunities, joy, and quality of life.
> (Haagerup, 2008)

Reading the column today when constructive journalism has become a household name in many newsrooms and classrooms around the world, several things come to mind. One is that this column contains very few examples of what constructive journalism is, could be, and should be. The same is true of the first works by Cathrine Gyldensted. In their first publications, the two founders are for good reasons forced to refer to journalists and editors who label their work under other names – if they label their work at all. It is also noteworthy that there is no mention of a "constructive journalism" in the column from 2008. Haagerup repeatedly refers to "constructive news," but that this could entail another form of journalism altogether is not clear in 2008. This point relates to a third symptomatic thing about the column. "Constructive news" is presented as something that entails a minor change in journalistic practice: supplementing existing news criteria with a new criterion for what is constructive (Haagerup, 2008).

What news to include – and exclude – for publication in the news media has been of prime importance since the nineteenth and twentieth centuries, where the views-papers were gradually replaced by newspapers (see Chapter 2), and political representatives, professors, and other professionals who had manned the newsrooms were gradually replaced by a new profession who specialized in getting and spreading the news. Some of the very first textbooks about journalism discuss this issue at length, for example, the textbook *The Practice of Journalism* (1922/1911) co-written by Walter Williams and a colleague from the first journalism school in the US (this is also the book in which the Journalist's Creed is included in later editions). The issue also became a popular object of study as research in journalism gradually developed, and as Haagerup and others have since pointed out, the very first researchers to write about the criteria for news selection – and rejection – noted the propensity for the news media to focus on problems.

One of these pioneering researchers, Johan Galtung, was in 2019 invited as speaker at an international conference hosted by Constructive Institute. On this occasion, Galtung reminded the participants that he and his co-writer, Maria Ruge, already in their very first scholarly article about news criteria had noted that the traditional and generally used news criteria will result in emphasis on "negativity," and "conflict will be emphasized, conciliation not" (1965, 84). The first list of news criteria compiled by Johan Galtung and Maria Ruge contained 12 "factors" that could explain what journalists selected – and rejected – as news stories. This list has been discussed many times in scholarly circles, and new lists have been drawn up by later generations of journalistic researchers – and at times also practitioners – because the list-makers believe their new works are better calibrated to account for different types of news, news formats, and news platforms. Indeed, one of the first fellows at Constructive Institute, Gerd Maria May, has also in recent years introduced a list of constructive news criteria (May, 2020).[2]

However, the founders did little in the first years to effectively control how "constructive" was defined more precisely. But when studying the column from 2008 closer, it is evident that Haagerup refers to *what could work*, when it comes to solving societal problems (e.g., in the form of the news story about how hospitals have found a solution to counter stress), and *what already works* (e.g., in the form of the news story about a majority of Danes who believe they have the job of their dreams). Cathrine Gyldensted's first work

66 *Practices of constructive journalism*

points to the same duality in terms of what constructive journalism entails. With inspiration from positive psychology, that is, shifting focus from what does not work to what works, Gyldensted introduces the concept of "positive journalism." In positive journalism, practitioners have a responsibility to document and present "another reality" to audiences than the world we know from negative reporting (Gyldensted & Bjerre, 2014, 27). Haagerup does not seem to use this concept himself in any of his works, but especially in his first publications, Haagerup refers to research that has shown that journalists fail to offer a complete view of the world, since they only focus on what goes wrong and neglect to inform audiences about "what goes well."

In her later works, Gyldensted makes a clearer distinction between "positive journalism" and "constructive journalism" (Gyldensted, 2015, 13; McIntyre & Gyldensted, 2017, 1022), and this aspect of reporting *what already works* seems to figure less prominently in Haagerup's later works, whereas *what could work* in the form of possible solutions and inspiration comes more to the forefront. As constructive journalism in time becomes something journalists, editors, and owners of news organizations not only read about but also attempt to practice – occasionally or continuously – it becomes clearer that the practice of constructive journalism affects not only what news stories are *selected* but also how these stories are *presented*. The two processes are connected, since what is selected affects what can ultimately be presented to audiences, and what needs to be presented affects what is selected. However, as constructive journalism has developed, it has become apparent that there are four approaches to the practice of journalism when we take "problems" and "potentials" into account: journalists can focus on (1) problems, (2) potentials, (3) problems and potentials, and (4) potentials and problems (see Figure 4.1).

The story that should have been about the "Lene effect" is telling when it comes to rooting out the important differences between these approaches. Haagerup's first point is that traditional news is based on something that contains a problem (1) to somebody, somewhere. This is why a report showing

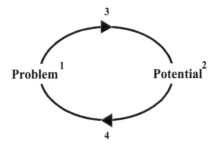

Figure 4.1 Four approaches to the selection and presentation of problems and potentials.

Practices of constructive journalism 67

0 percent unemployment among immigrant women is not considered news by his own journalists and editors. Haagerup offers two reasons why pointing to a potential (2) should also be considered relevant news. First, the employment rate is an example of something that already works, and a news story about a 0 percent unemployment rate could offer a more complete picture of the real world. As both Haagerup and Gyldensted mention, it is akin to watching the world with both eyes, so readers, listeners, and viewers get an understanding of the positive as well as the negative. "We need both, often in a shifting, alternating balance," as Gyldensted has put it (2015, 8). Second, the report refers to something – "the Lene effect" – that could work in other municipalities.

This news story, which contained two potentials (what works and what could work), was never produced. However, Haagerup has suggested in later publications that potentials should not be presented without an accompanying problem. His point, which becomes increasingly clear in his later works, is not that problems (1) should not be presented, but rather that possible potentials (2), such as "the Lene effect," should be acknowledged, so that a news story presents problems first and then potentials (3). Haagerup has expressed this in different ways over the years. Constructive journalism should "add a layer" or an "additional step" to problems and "move beyond the five w's (what, when, where, who, why) to what-now," and although the wording changes, the point stays the same (Haagerup, 2014, 2017). Gyldensted makes a similar point. She notes that potentials can be presented on their own to offer a more complete picture of the world (2), and she notes the importance of including "C's: the conflict, the crisis and the complications" (2015, 47) that should precede the "constructive" part of the news story (3).

Gyldensted acknowledges that this combination of problems and potentials (3) has little news value in itself. In *From Mirrors to Movers* (2015), she refers specifically to David Merritt, one of the founders of the public journalism movement, who noted that the journalistic expertise in finding problems "should have been a plateau from which the profession moved on to even greater heights," but as it were, "finding problems turned out to be a peak" (cf. Gyldensted, 2015, 58). That is, finding problems became an end in itself rather than a means to seeking possible solutions. This has been an important point for both movements in the late nineteenth and late twentieth centuries. A memorable phrase from another supporter of public journalism states that "journalism's role of providing information is only the beginning of the task" (E.J. Dionne cf. Campbell, 1999, xv), and a hundred years earlier, William Randolph Hearst's *The World* criticized newspapers that were content "with pointing out existing evils or giving warning of impending dangers. They gave the alarm and whether it was heeded or not was no concerns of theirs." Believing that newspapers had a greater responsibility and a more active role to play, *The Journal* argued that "when things are going wrong" newspapers "should set them right."

The fourth approach is characterized by a turn of presentation. Here potentials are presented first only to be problematized afterward (4). This approach has emerged in the wake of the constructive journalism movement and is also promoted by journalists – most often from the US and the UK – who label their work "solutions journalism." This potential–problem approach is also apparent in what the Solution Journalism Network has described as the pivotal "four steps":

> Response: Focuses on a response to a social problem — and on how that response has worked, or why it hasn't. 2) Insight: Shows what can be learned from a response and why it matters to a newsroom's audience. 3) Evidence: Provides data or qualitative results that indicate effectiveness (or lack thereof). And 4) Limitations: Places responses in context; doesn't shy away from revealing shortcomings.
>
> (Solutions Journalism Network, 2023)

Throughout this process, the solution – in this four-step model dubbed "response" – is in every step of the process critically investigated, scrutinized, and problematized.

Relevant issues for constructive journalism

As the idea of constructive journalism became popular, considerations about how to practice it, more generally, and what issues to cover constructively, more specifically, came to the forefront. Such considerations did not trouble the first generations of active journalists, editors, and owners of news organizations much, as they sought to solve a seemingly endless variety of problems. *The Journal*, for one, worked in accordance with Hearst's so-called theory that "when things are going wrong," a newspaper "should itself set them right, if possible," and there were many problems for *The Journal*, *The World*, and other like-minded newspapers to set right in the late nineteenth century. Crime, corruption, and the much-discussed incarceration of the daughter of a Cuban rebel leader with strong American ties were some of the problems to which *The Journal* and its competitors sought solutions. Many of the problems were commonly shared societal problems, others were more personal and individual, and researchers have since developed typologies to describe the different types of crusades and campaigns that journalists, on both sides of the Atlantic, embarked on (see, e.g., Chalaby, 2000).[3]

Close to a century later, journalistic practitioners gave more thought to what problems to cover, but neither the movement in the late twentieth century nor the movement in the early twenty-first century was precise about what issues to cover and what not to cover. Indeed, some supporters have suggested that constructive journalism is simply an extension of more traditional problem-oriented journalism, where every problem that is relevant in traditional journalism should simply be accompanied by a constructive approach. "Constructive journalism completes the circle with what is missing, when problems have been described," two former fellows at Constructive Institute, Kristina Lund Jørgensen and Jakob Risbro, write in their textbook *Constructive Journalism: From Idea to Story* (2021, 36). However, when studying the many international examples that supporters of constructive journalism – and of solutions journalism – have produced in recent years, some issues seem to be covered more intense than others.

In order to understand why some issues are more popular than others, it can be useful to build on the scholarly work of Daniel Hallin. Based on studies of how the American press covered the Vietnam war in the 1970s, Hallin concluded that the work of journalists can best be understood on the basis of three so-called "regions" or "spheres": the sphere of consensus, the sphere of legitimate controversy, and the sphere of deviance.[4] According to Hallin, the sphere of consensus encompasses issues that journalists do not consider controversial, and within this sphere, "journalists do not feel compelled either to present opposing views or to remain disinterested observers" (1989, 116–117). This is precisely what Hallin found happened in the first years of coverage when the U.S. news media did not problematize the war efforts. The sphere of legitimate controversy, on the other hand, relates to issues where "objectivity and balance reign" (1989, 116), and Hallin concluded that as opposition to the war developed in the political establishment and among the general public, journalists started asking more critical questions and presenting opposing views. The result was legitimate controversy over the war.

Finally, beyond the sphere of legitimate controversy lies the sphere of deviance, and this is the realm of those things (issues, topics, persons, organizations, etc.) journalists "reject as unworthy" of being presented to a wider audience (1989, 117). Together these three spheres marks a spectrum of acceptability, and Hallin's typology was originally introduced to help describe and discuss how the journalism coverage of the Vietnam war developed. But with a few moderations, Hallin's model and its inherent concepts can help describe and discuss the selection processes in constructive journalism as well (see Figure 4.2). This moderated version builds on Hallin's work, where the consensual sphere includes issues that journalists generally agree to accept for news presentation; the controversial sphere includes issues that journalists might be in conflict about, but where some journalists and news media still present them; and finally, the deviant sphere pertains to issues that journalists agree to reject for news presentation. All three types of issues are related to two different types of journalism: the passive journalism with a focus on problems, and the active journalism where potentials are in focus.

This modified model is meant to illustrate two different conceptions about what issues are worthy for news selection, and it can be used in several ways. First and foremost, the model can be used to compare the relevance of news

70 *Practices of constructive journalism*

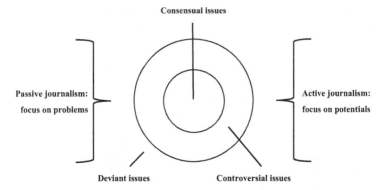

Figure 4.2 Constructive journalism's consensual, controversial, and deviant issues. Adapted from *The Uncensored War: The Media and Vietnam* by Daniel C. Hallin, 1986.

stories in different journalistic contexts. To take one example, the story about the "Lene effect" was considered a deviant issue by a journalist and editor working for the Danish Broadcasting Company. The story was not considered relevant since it did not contain a problem, people in the newsroom concluded (Haagerup, 2008). However, in constructive journalism, where potentials (what works well and what might work) are the primary focus, this story would have been produced and broadcast, Haagerup suggests. The model can also be used as a framework for discussing the relevance of issues within each of these journalistic paradigms. Hallin's original work grew out of on the left-hand side of the model, since that was the prevailing journalistic paradigm at the time, and he found that war coverage developed from the inside out as well as from the outside in.

In the first period of the war, few if any in the mainstream news media questioned the war efforts, but as discontent developed among the public and in the political establishment in Washington DC, it became more legitimate for journalists to shine a light on the problems with the war effort. Hallin's study also showed that some issues – and by implication, also some persons and organizations – were considered deviant those first years. The national broadcasters in the US did, for example, not "make time available to Communists or to the Communist viewpoints."[5] That changed later, and in effect new political viewpoints moved from being deviant to controversial. The differentiation between the three types of issues continues to offer a telling framework for studies of journalists and journalism that focus on problems. In political journalism that are still some issues that in some countries are considered deviant (e.g., do Danish journalists, in general, not write about marital sidesteps, affairs, etc.?), while there is widespread consensus about other issues (e.g., in sports journalism, where it is OK for national, regional, and local media to have a more positive tone toward to the home teams).

In the context of this book, it is particular relevant to look at the three types of issues from the right-hand side of the model, and while debates over constructive journalism continue, some researchers have suggested that some issues seldom, if ever, cause controversy. Unni From and Nete Nørgaard Kristensen have shown that constructive journalism has much in common with service journalism, where the news media presents various types of "news you can use" (2018). In service journalism, the news media publicly addresses the concerns of private lives, and in the words of one of the scholarly pioneers within this field, "Through the format of service journalism, journalists express that they are at the service of their audiences. They stress that they are ready to contribute to solving everyday problems and providing the pleasures of consumption" (Eide, 2017, 199).

From and Nørgaard, rightly, stipulate that there is a difference between the service journalism that has been a permanent feature in many news media for centuries and the constructive journalism that Haagerup and Gyldensted envision. In all of their publications, Haagerup and Gyldensted write about the issues related to hard news, whereas service journalism is rooted in soft news, such as lifestyle journalism. Nonetheless, it is remarkable that even some of the most critical journalists and editors work for news media, where constructive stories take up space and have done so for centuries. There is, in other words, a widespread consensus about the value of constructive journalism as long as the presentation of potentials is used in certain ways. Other issues – and approaches – are more controversial or even considered deviant by proponents, supporters, and practitioners of more active types of journalism. While there were few if any issues that the active journalists, editors, and owners of news organizations at the turn of the last century would not engage actively in, later generations of active journalism have been more restrained.

One of the founders of public journalism, Jay Rosen, believed that journalism could in "certain cases intervene in the service of broad public values without compromising its integrity" (1996, 13), but as researchers have shown, the issues that became the basis of public journalism projects were restricted. These projects, generally, sought to solve problems that were universally acknowledged by people outside the newsrooms (health, racism, crime, traffic incidents, unemployment, poverty, lack of participation in elections, etc.), and although there were controversies over what might be the best solutions to the problems, the problems themselves were less debated. The same approach has been the case for the constructive journalism movement, and Haagerup has stated that the starting point for constructive journalism should be "well documented problems" and "important issues facing society" (see, e.g., 2017, 146), and he has added that news stories about what works already or could work in the future should be presented just as neutral and objective as in traditional journalism.

Hallin's original study is a reminder that the spectrum of acceptability can change over time, and this has certainly also been the case when it comes to active journalism. Some practitioners who normally adhere to the traditional journalistic paradigm have in time come to believe that there are some issues that warrant a more active approach. One such example is the issue of climate problems, where several news organizations have supplemented their focus on problems with a focus on potentials. One such example is mentioned by Gyldensted in *From Mirrors to Movers* (2015). "The treat to our species is so severe that this is one of those rare subjects where you can move from reporting to campaigning," the former editor-in-chief of *The Guardian* explains in an interview in the book (2015, 154). This belief led him to ask his staff a series of questions that could help guide their journalism.

> What can we do that lifts this to a new generation, beyond something they are bored to read about or cannot bear to read about? What can we do to force them to sit up and pay attention – and may even act?
>
> (Gyldensted, 2015, 153)

This is a telling example of how the spectrum of acceptability can change over time and space and even in relation to different issues. If not continuously, then occasionally journalists, editors, and owners of news organizations can come to find that some issues are better covered by focusing on the potentials than the problems, and in the process, issues might also move inside and out or outside and in in relation to the model above. Hallin reminds us that such shifts between what he termed "spheres" not only depends on what takes place inside newsroom, but also on what occurs outside the newsrooms. Incidents, accidents, and actions of persons, organizations, and institutions are important influencing factors, and the life stories of both founders of the constructive movement are testament to the importance of such external factors. Their reflections about the roles and responsibilities of journalism have also been prompted by what they have experienced as part of their work. Cathrine Gyldensted, for example, points to a meeting with a homeless woman, that made her search for another approach to journalism (2015, 10), where stories she would never have considered relevant before now became something she pursued.

Relevant sources for constructive journalism

"Kill those victims," Cathrine Gyldensted and Malene Bjerre order readers of their textbook about constructive journalism (2014, 5). The morbid statement was originally coined by Ingrid Thörnqvist, an editor from the Swedish Broadcasting Corporation, and the implication is less dramatic than it might seem. Thörnqvist and the two authors hope for fewer news stories where persons, organizations, or nations are presented as journalistic casualties.

This call echoes that of the founders of the two previous movements from the nineteenth and twentieth centuries. In the case of public journalism, Jay Rosen suggested that journalists "address people as citizens, potential participants in public affairs, rather than victims or spectators" (1999, 22). Close to a century before the birth of the public journalism movement, scores of active journalists and editors showed how that could be done, since the inclusion of members of the public was important for them as well.

Pulitzer's campaign to finance the pedestal of the Statue of Liberty is perhaps one of the most famous and successful examples of how newspapers at the time enlisted the help of ordinary people. Pulitzer asked the citizens of New York City for help, and once the funding was secured, he published the names of all contributors – many of them were children who contributed a penny – in *The World*. All this suggests that private citizens can appear in very different ways in the news media. Sometimes they participate in the news media as *problem-holders*, or as "victims" or "cases," and Thörnqvist noticed that this often happened whenever the Swedish Broadcasting Corporation presented news stories from third world countries. At other times, private citizens appear as the opposite: *problem-solvers*. While there is much typecasting in journalism, the important point here is that journalists can cast and direct news sources, so that they are used to perform particular functions in journalism. This is illustrated in Figure 4.3 in a slightly modified version of a model for sourcing practices in journalism (Bro, 2018).

The leftmost column lists examples of typical sources in contemporary news media, and the top row lists three roles the news sources can play. Just as journalists can play different roles – for example, regarding how passive and active they are, and how representative and deliberative their perspective is (see Chapter 1) – they can assign different roles to news sources and present them in the form of so-called "stereotypes." "Stereotypes" were originally wooden, metallic, or other types of plates with engraved symbols that printers could place together letter after letter, line after line, sentence after sentence,

Roles / Sources	Marker		Translator		Actor	
	Problem	Potential	Problem	Potential	Problem	Potential
Citizens						
Researchers						
Politicians						
… etc.						

Figure 4.3 Sourcing practices in constructive journalism.

and page after page to speed up the printing processes. Since the early twentieth century, the concept crossed professional boundaries and has also been used in journalism. One of the first to use the concept was Walter Lippmann, a journalist at *The World* who later became a worldwide syndicated political commentator and Pulitzer Prize winner.

Lippmann is perhaps mostly known for his book *Public Opinion* (1922), called "the founding book of modern journalism" (Carey, 1987). Referring directly to the way journalists use stereotypes in their work, Lippmann notes that people "tend to perceive that which we have picked out in the form stereotyped for us" (1997/1922, 55). The three roles – markers, translators, and actors – are examples of such stereotypes in journalism. The "marker" typically refers to a person who can personify a problem or potential. Markers are at times also described as "cases," and when they personify a problem, journalists may refer to them as "victims." This happens frequently in traditional problem-based journalism, and in one of his publications, Haagerup exemplifies how journalists might search for sources to a news story about retirement. "Can we drum up a dentist who feels disappointed and angry at the prospect of not being able to retire at the age he or she has been looking forward to retiring for years? Or can we find someone with a manual labor job whose working life has been so demanding that it would be hard on them to continue to work into old age?" (Haagerup, 2017, 65).

Haagerup criticizes traditional journalism and journalists for always looking for "victims" who have experienced problems or who can personify something problematic (2017, 65), and private citizens are often typecast as markers with whom audiences can identify – identification being a classic news criterion. But as proponents, supporters, and practitioners of constructive journalism suggest, people can also mark potentials, for example, Lene in "the Lene effect." As Gyldensted and Bjerre note, not only individuals can represent potentials:

> So now take the lives of those victims. Instead, go out and look for the multitude of stories that exist about people who have found meaning in life. Companies that have broken new ground and developed surprising collaborations. Countries that have found good solutions to difficult conflicts. Stories that point the way to a better world.
> (Gyldensted & Bjerre, 2014, 5)

While markers are used by journalists to exemplify individual and personal aspects of problems and potentials, translators are used to offer perspectives on a more universal and general level, for example, what a problem amounts to in the rest of the country or the rest of the world. The first generation of journalists, editors, and owners who attempted to do more than simply present problems used translators proactively to persuade others to act, because they could attest to the fact that it was not only a few people who experienced problems – or had discovered a potential – but many people who could potentially be affected. Around the turn of the last century, translators could take the form of dentists, doctors, police commissioners, and others with knowledge out of the ordinary, but today, translators are typically university researchers and other experts who possess scientific and research-based knowledge that can translate problems and potentials.

The third and final role is the actor. Actors are persons who have done something that journalists believe poses either a problem or a potential, or they are persons whom journalists believe should do something in the future. "What will you do to solve this problem?" is a typical question asked by journalists who are not content with simply presenting problems but also attempt to prompt others to act. This approach has been fine-tuned over the years by active journalists, and to heighten the pressure on people to act, they typically introduce one or several markers and translators, so that other people can identify with the problems and learn about the general ramifications of the problems. In much traditional journalism, actors in news stories are representatives of the public, for example, politicians.

This typology of stereotypes in the news media is helpful for understanding differences and similarities between constructive journalism and more traditional types of journalism. The typology is also useful in terms of distinguishing between the different movements in the history of journalism, where journalists, editors, and owners of news organizations have more or less actively attempted to "move" the world – to paraphrase the title of one of Gyldensted's books (2015). Seen through the lenses of this typology, constructive journalism calls on practitioners of the craft to not only present news sources who can attest to problems – as markers, translators, and actors – but include news sources who can point to potentials, that is, something that has worked in the past or could work in the present or future. Both Haagerup and Gyldensted include this future perspective in their works almost from the beginning.[6] In the Danish anthology published in 2012, Haagerup criticizes the traditional news media for only focusing on the past and the present by asking, "What has happened? Who is responsible? Who are the victims?" (2012b, 44).

Haagerup calls on journalists to make societal problems the starting point of any news story, after which the journalists can start searching for ways in which people can solve these problems in the future. He wants journalists to inspire decision-makers and the public with possible solutions. Whom the constructive journalists consider actors in their news stories marks an important difference between the movements from the nineteenth, twentieth, and twenty-first centuries, and constructive journalism may have more in common with the active journalism at the turn of the last century. While public journalists believed in, including the public, the proponents, supporters, and practitioners of "journalism that does things", "action journalism" and associated concepts attempted to prompt action among both private citizens and authoritative decision-makers. Solving the problems was more important than who solved the problems, and sometimes journalists and editors took part in the solutions.

Likewise, the founders and later practitioners of constructive journalism do not seem to hold strong opinions – particularly in the first years of the movement – about who is included as actors with a potential. In her early works, Gyldensted describes how not only individuals but also organizations and nations can help solve important societal problems. One example is the inspiration behind the solutions journalism movement. Tina Rosenberg was working as a reporter for *The New York Times* on a story about the AIDS pandemic, and after a source told her how Brazil had effectively fought the pandemic, she decided to change her perspective from problems to solutions. "I knew it and, fortunately, so did my editor. That story from Brazil would be a far better story than let-us-go-to-Malawi-and-show-how-everyone-is-dying story," Rosenberg explains in *From Mirrors to Movers* (Gyldensted, 2014, 83). The solutions that this new approach brought with it were not as much directed toward what members of the public could do as what politicians could accomplish on a national and an international level.

Among the examples of what Haagerup considers constructive journalism are also projects where the problem-holders are private citizens – often cast in the role of markers with a problem – and the problem-solvers are politicians. On several occasions, Haagerup has participated in constructive journalism projects where politicians – mayors and members of parliament – have been summoned to contemplate and late decide on the best solutions to problems. In one such project, six Danish mayors had to spend 24 hours together in a vacation home to find solutions to problems with tourism (Haagerup, 2014, 58). Casting representatives of the public rather than the public as the actors who are responsible for solving problems also makes sense from a practical perspective. As research on the results of the public journalism movement has shown, private citizens may not have the required reaction time, level of reflection, and radius of action.

First, it can be difficult for journalists working with deadlines to get in contact with private citizens, while it is easier to locate politicians. Second, individual citizens may not have given problems and their possible solutions much thought, whereas journalists can easily identify, locate, and contact other news sources who are already aware of the problems and potential solutions. Third, individual citizens can only do so much, while politicians, company executives, and others can enlist more manpower, money, and other means to solve problems (Bro, 2019). "[P]ositioning citizens as political actors and not just as spectators," as one former editor-in-chief and supporter of the public journalism movement called on his colleagues in the news media to do,[7] can be challenging, which helps explain why active journalists – in the past and in the present – at times find it easier to approach representatives of the public when they want to prompt action and solve societal problems.

Expanding ambitions and aspirations for constructive journalism

From the initial, modest call in a column in a Danish newspaper to introducing a new news criterion, constructive journalism now encompasses many other elements. Gyldensted, who has traveled much of the world to introduce the practice of constructive journalism to present and future journalists, conducted master classes on best practice, set up programs at journalism schools, and has widened the scope in recent years in terms of what journalism could – and should – do. In her book *Did You Get Smarter?* (2020), she describes and discusses how journalists – and others – can improve public conversation. Although the book also discusses how that might help "move" the world, better means and methods for public communication are here seen as an end in itself. Haagerup has also widened his perspective and expanded the scope for what he today considers crucial for constructive journalism. In his latest publications and on the website of Constructive Institute, the type of journalism he helped introduce is now based on three pillars:

(1) Focus on solutions: Not only expose the problems, but also look for possible solutions. (2) Cover nuances: Strive for the best obtainable version of the truth. See the world with both eyes. (3) Promote democratic conversation: Engage in and facilitate debate, include people in the community.

These three pillars are presented as the "foundation of constructive journalism practice," and they all relate to the "main mission: to contribute to democracy."

All this amounts to a wide-ranging and far-reaching development for the constructive journalism movement: from a column in a newspaper in Denmark to newsrooms – and now increasingly classrooms – around much of the world, and from a modest ambition to the introduction of a new, constructive news criterion to a self-proclaimed contribution to democracy. These expanding ambitions and aspirations for constructive journalism certainly pose challenges, as the previous chapters have shown. While it was unclear from the beginning what "constructive" entailed, the complexity only seems to have increased as the principles and now also practices have developed. This stands in starch contrast to a movement like solutions journalism that has narrower focus. While the movements share a belief in the first pillar, constructive journalism has come to encompass two additional pillars.

In all fairness it should be mentioned that the US-based Solution Journalism Network has also introduced the concept of pillars, but all of these four pillars relate to the first pillar in Haagerup's construction.[8] The use of "pillars" is a telling example of the different reach and relevance of the two movements, and while some journalistic practitioners and researchers in the past have used constructive journalism and solutions journalism synonymously,

78 Practices of constructive journalism

this makes less sense today (see, e.g., Lough & McIntyre, 2021). However, the expanding ambitions and aspirations also offer opportunities for constructive journalism. The range of problems and potentials, which constructive journalism has come to encompass today, has attracted interest from persons and organizations outside of the news media, including foundations and other funding bodies – all of which have helped support a fellowship program at Constructive Institute in Denmark, annual conferences, master classes, and seminars around the world and other initiatives that support the continual development and implementation of constructive journalism methods, tools, and techniques.[9]

Notes

1 Some models have been developed specifically to accommodate the practice of constructive journalism, and as evidenced in the previous chapters, the founders, Ulrik Haagerup and Cathrine Gyldensted, have been especially productive here. But other models have been developed by fellows from the Constructive Institute, and two such noteworthy examples are the so-called STEP-model (Solutions, Trust, Engagement, and Perspective) by former fellow, Gerd Maria May, which is presented in her book about constructive journalism in 2021, and the Constructive Compass, which was developed by the two later fellows, Kristina Lund Sørensen and Jacob Risbro (2021). Other models come from different fields and have been modified to fit constructive journalism. One prime example of this is a model used in positive psychology that Gyldensted has included in several of her works. This PERMA-model points to five elements related to human well-being: Positive emotion, Engagement, Relationships, Meaning, and Accomplishment. Today, many news organizations have themselves started producing manuals, checklists, toolboxes, and other guidelines that can supplement what is already available, when it comes to the possible tools, techniques, and methods of constructive journalism. But several news organizations have also developed their own manuals and models. These include international news organizations like the BBC, national news organizations like the Norwegian Broadcast Corporation, and regional news organizations like the Danish TV station, TV2 Funen.
2 Gerd Maria May, a former fellow at Constructive Institute, is the author of a book in Danish about constructive journalism (2021). The book introduces the so-called "STEP-model," where each of the four letters in the acronym represents a topic that should be addressed when doing constructive journalism: Solutions, Trust, Engagement, and Perspective. Each of the four can be seen as a news criterion.
3 For example, Jacob A. Riis embarked on a project to help a lonely, elderly lady, and the journalists considered their public work a success when they could deliver a parrot. The example is from the article "Communicative Networks", where there are a number of examples of how Jacob A. Riis helped with practical problems. The New York *World* referred to his office as "the mecca of a constant procession", where people with problems and people with potential means to solve the problems would pass by, and in his career, he helped distribute everything from wheelchairs and baby carriages to parcels of clothes and a parrot to a lonely, elderly woman (Bro, 2003, 530).
4 It is important to note that this was, in part, due to regulations. Hallin notes that it was written "into the FCC's guidelines" (1986, 117).
5 Hallin stressed that there could be internal gradations between the three spheres. There are "internal gradations" and "fuzzy boundaries", he has noted (1989, 117–118).

6 In her book, *From Mirrors to Movers* (2015), Gyldensted quote the former editor-in-chief of *The Guardian*, Alan Rusbridger, for making a similar point: "Journalism looks too much in the rear-view-mirror" (cf. Gyldensted, 2015, 18).
7 This call to journalists was made by Cole C. Campbell, former editor-in-chief of the *St. Louis Post-Dispatch* (Campbell, 1999, xviii).
8 The four pillars of solutions journalism are Response, Insight, Evidence, and Limitations. The Solution Journalism Network describes them as follows: "(1) A solutions story focuses on a *response* to a social problem – and how that response has worked or why it hasn't. (2) The best solutions reporting distills the lessons that makes the response relevant and accessible to others. In other words, it offers *insight*. (3) Solutions journalism looks for evidence – data or qualitative results that show effectiveness (or lack thereof). Solutions stories are up front with audiences about that evidence – what it tells us and what it doesn't. A particularly innovative response can be a good story even without much evidence – but the reporter has to be transparent about the lack, and about why the response is newsworthy anyway. (4) Solutions stories reveal a response's shortcomings. No response is perfect, and some work well for one community but may fail in others. A responsible reporter covers what doesn't work about it, and places the response in context. Reporting on *limitations*, in other words, is essential." The four pillars are presented on the website of The Solutions Journalism Network (https://www.solutionsjournalism.org – accessed March 1, 2023).
9 This is another place where the constructive journalism movement resembles that of the public journalism movement. One of the observers of the public journalism movement, Barbie Zelizer, has written about the extensive support given to the public journalism movement over the 1990s: "Funding institutes such as the Kettering Foundation, the Twentieth Century Fund, the Poynter Institute for Media Studies, the Knight Foundation, and the Pew Charitable Trusts have lauded public journalism, funneling substantial monies, institutional attention, and other resources towards its development" (Zelizer, 1999, 153).

References

Bro, Peter (2003) "Communicative networks." *Journalism Studies* 5 (4): 525–535.

Bro, Peter (2018) *Models of Journalism: The Function and Influencing Factors*. London: Routledge.

Bro, Peter (2019) "Public or civic journalism." In *The International Encyclopedia of Journalism Studies*, edited by T. P. Vos and F. Hanusch. New York: Wiley-Blackwell.

Campbell, Cole C. (1999) "Foreword: Journalism as a democratic act." In *The Idea of Public Journalism*, edited by Theodore L. Glasser, xiii–xxix, New York: Guildford Press.

Campbell, W. Joseph (2006) *The Year That Defined American Journalism: 1897 and the Clash of Paradigms*. New York: Routledge.

Carey, James W. (1987) "The press and public discourse." *The Center Magazine* 20: 4–16.

Chalaby, Jean K. (2000) "Northcliffe's journalism." *Media History* 6 (1): 33–44.

Eide, Martin (2017) "The culture of service journalism." In *Cultural Journalism in the Nordic Countries*, edited by Nete Nørgaard Kristensen and Kristina Riegert, 195–204, Göteborg: Nordicom.

From, Unni and Nete Nørgaard Kristensen (2018) "Rethinking Constructive journalism by means of service journalism." *Journalism Practice* 12 (6): 714–729.

Galtung, Johan and Marie Ruge (1965) "The structure of foreign news." *Journal of Peace Research* 2 (1): 64–91.Gyldensted, Cathrine (2015) *From Mirrors to Movers:*

Five Elements of Positive Psychology in Constructive Journalism. Charleston, SC: Group Publishing.

Gyldensted, Cathrine (2020) *Blev du Klogere: Sådan Forbedrer du den Offentlige Samtale* [Did You Get Smarter: How to Improve Public Conversation]. København: Forlaget Højskolerne.

Gyldensted, Cathrine and Malene Bjerre (2014) *Håndbog i Konstruktiv Journalistic* [Handbook in Constructive Journalism]. Århus: Ajour.

Haagerup, Ulrik (2008) "Konstruktive nyheder" [Constructive News]. *Politiken*, December 6.

Haagerup, Ulrik (2012a) *En Konstruktiv Nyhed* [A Constructive News Story]. Århus: Ajour.

Haagerup, Ulrik (2012b) "Et opgør med nyhedsvanen [A showdown with the news habit]." In *En Konstruktiv Nyhed* [A Constructive News Story], edited by Ulrik Haagerup, 21–46, Århus: Ajour.

Haagerup, Ulrik (2014) *Constructive News: How to Save the Media and Democracy with Journalism of Tomorrow*. New York: InnoVatio Publishing.

Haagerup, Ulrik (2017) *Constructive News: How to Save the Media and Democracy with Journalism of Tomorrow.* Aarhus, Denmark: Aarhus University Press.

Hallin, Daniel C. (1986) *The Uncensored War: The Media and Vietnam*. Oakland: University of California Press.

Jørgensen, Kristina Lund and Jakob Risbro (2021) *Konstruktiv Journalistik: Fra Ide Til Historie* [Constructive Journalism: From Idea to Story]. Århus: Forlaget Ajour.

Lippmann, Walter (1997/1922) *Public Opinion*. New York: First Free Press.

Lough, Kyser, and Karen McIntyre (2021) "A systematic review of constructive and solutions journalism research." *Journalism*. Advance Online Publication.

May, Gerd Maria (2020) *Fra Tårn Til Torv* [From Tower to Square]. Odense: Syddansk Universitetsforlag.

McIntyre, Karen, and Cathrine Gyldensted (2017) "Constructive journalism: Applying positive psychology techniques to news production." *The Journal of Media Innovations* 4 (2): 20–34.

Rosen, Jay (1996) *Getting the Connections Right.* New York: The Twentieth Century Fund Press.

Rosen, Jay (1999) "The action of the idea". In *The Idea of Public Journalism*, edited by Theodore L. Glasser, 21–48, New York: Guilford Press.

Williams, Walter and Frank L. Martin (1922/1911) *The Practice of Journalism*. Columbia: Missouri Book Services.

Zelizer, Barbie (1999) "Making the neighborhood work: The improbabilities of public journalism." In *The Idea of Public Journalism*, edited by Theodore Glasser, 152–172, New York: Guildford Press.

5 Conclusion

Some of the most iconic figures in journalism history have worked in the belief that the news media should do more than present problems. Around the turn of the last century, journalists, editors, and owners of newspapers, such as William Randolph Hearst, Joseph Pulitzer, William Stead, Lord Northcliffe, and Henrik Cavling, to name but a few, believed that journalism should – continuously or occasionally – help solve societal problems. If fame and fortune are measures of success, many of these early promoters of active journalism have been immensely successful. Renowned newspaper publishers, such as Hearst, Pulitzer, and Northcliffe, amassed fortunes that made them some of the world's richest men, and many journalists and editors who actively worked to help society solve its problems around the turn of the last century also made names for themselves. To this day, their names appear in textbooks about journalism and adorn prize diplomas for journalistic excellence, and some of them even lend their names to buildings at journalism schools.[1] However, the journalistic principles and practices that these iconic figures promoted in their lifetime – and indeed believed would become the future of journalism – did not become a more permanent fixture after their death.

Hearst proclaimed that "new journalism," "action journalism," and "journalism that does things" were "the final stage in the evolution of the modern journalism. Ever boastful, Hearst even noted: "The journalism that does things has come to stay. There is still room for the old journals, however. They can occupy themselves in telling what the new journals are doing." Pulitzer claimed that "(t)he power to mould the future … will in the hands of the journalists of future generations," and he called for a new generation of journalists who would take active responsibility for the public welfare. They were not alone. In England, newspaper magnates such as Lord Northcliffe crusaded for change, and William Stead – one of the original sources of inspiration for Hearst's and Pulitzer's so-called "new journalism" – wrote with passion about the need for "journalism-as-government." Stead believed the press was in a better position than any other institutions, organizations, and individuals to help society solve its most pertinent problems. In Denmark, Cavling, who has been credited with initiating a "press revolution" in Denmark and neighboring

DOI: 10.4324/9781003403098-5

countries, also advocated for the "action journalism" that could help bring newspapers and the public closer together. "And it is on this relationship, which is still only at its beginning, that newspapers' development will largely depend," Cavling wrote in 1909, when the newspaper he had become editor-in-chief for celebrated its 25th anniversary.

The immediate future of journalism turned out differently than these men had envisioned, and throughout most of the twentieth century, a passive type of journalism evolved and was practiced in the newsroom on both sides of the Atlantic.[2] To be sure, these later generations of journalists still believed in the social responsibility of journalism (Bro & Gyldensted, 2021), but they, by and large, contented themselves with only presenting problems and then left it to people outside the news organizations to decide what to do about the problems, if anything at all. Naturally, there were exceptions. But when some news organizations embarked on solving problems, it was often in the form of charitable work that was separated from the journalistic work, and paradoxically, some of the journalistic prizes that were instituted in the twentieth century came to bear the names of the forerunners of the active, solution-focused journalism of the late nineteenth century. The Pulitzer Prize and the Cavling Prize have, for many decades, been awarded to practitioners of a more passive, problem-focused journalism, and as the previous chapters have shown, it was not really until the late twentieth century that more active types of journalism resurfaced on a larger scale.[3]

Under names such as public journalism, civic journalism, community journalism, and a host of other concepts, journalistic practitioners and researchers started experimenting with new, active types of journalism. These experiments spread through much of the world before dissolving. In part by design, because the founders from the outset hoped the experiments with public journalism – a name inspired by Pulitzer's call for a more public-spirited journalism a hundred years earlier – would simply evolve and become a part of regular journalism. In part by default, because the problem-solving approaches were widely discussed and criticized by other representatives from the more traditional types of journalism. In Denmark, where public journalism also became popular in the late twentieth century (Haas, 2007), a critical news director described some of the experiments as the most "perverted type of journalism" he had ever experienced (Bro, 2004). Critics in the US also debunked the new movement as "fix-it-journalism" (Frankel, 1995) called the supporters a "cult" and the resulting journalism a "menace" to the craft, and even supporters criticized the public journalism movement for the vagueness of its basic principles and practices.[4]

These years a new journalistic movement is once again spreading to newsrooms around the world – and increasingly to journalism schools and universities – and while there is much to be excited about as journalists, editors, and owners of news organizations again are experimenting with more active types of journalism, there are also warning signs. Because the things that caused the two previous movements to fail seems to be inherent in the constructive journalism movement, learn from past experiments and experiences. This chapter will draw on previous chapters to describe these warning signs, and discuss similarities and differences between the previous movements to do more than present problems and it will end with what we might learn from past experiences with experimenting with types of journalism.

Similarities and differences between active types of journalism

There are, to be sure, noteworthy differences between the three major movements in the history of journalism that have attempted to do more than present problems. The active journalism around the turn of the last century was not only "restless," as the journalism historian W. Joseph Campbell has reminded us. It was at times also "reckless" (2006, 87). Journalists, editors, and owners of newspapers in that era promoted and even took part in the actual problem-solving, because they believed they were in a better position than other institutions, organizations, and associations to solve problems. Pulitzer, Hearst, and Nortcliffe were also prone to publishing sensational news stories that later turned out to be on the edge of truth, and at times Hearst also used his own newspapers to promote and prompt his political agendas. Things were different a century later, where one of the founders of the public journalism movement, Davis Merritt, stated that "public journalism does not seek to join with or substitute itself for government" (Merritt, 1995, 142). But still, public journalism was by most accounts more active than the constructive journalism that since developed, and these three movements also differ in other important ways.

For many of the practitioners of public journalism, the inclusion of the public in journalism was not only considered means to help solve societal problems. Inclusion of the public and public deliberations, where both private citizens and authoritative decision-makers were invited to take part in the solution process, was an end in itself for some public journalists. Jay Rosen, who was another founder of the movement, noted at one point that "I do not believe journalists should be solving problems. I think they should be creating the capacity within the community to solve problems" (Rosen, 1999), and this marks another important difference between the movements. The inclusion of the public – as an end in itself or as a means to other ends – is a testament to the bottom-up approach in the public journalism movement, whereas the other movements, which preceded and succeeded public journalism, have been based more on a top-down process.[5] This was certainly the case with the journalism that does things, where Hearst, Pulitzer, Northcliffe, Stead, and Cavling often involved themselves directly in the news work.

In constructive journalism, the practitioners have also been cast as those in charge, but this has, in part, changed over the past years, where new constitutive elements have been added to the definitions of what constructive

84 Conclusion

journalism is. While some of the original elements have been defined in stricter terms as time has gone by – particularly when it comes to just how active constructive journalists could and should be (see Chapter 3) – other elements have been added. Both of the founders of the movements have begun to include a stronger focus on the inclusion of the public and the need for public deliberations. Today, one the founders of the constructive journalism movement, Ulrik Haagerup, illustrates and defines constructive journalism as a construction based on three pillars, where the third pillar calls on journalists to engage people and facilitate public debates. The other founder, Cathrine Gyldensted, has also, very recently, published a book about how to ensure better public debates (2020).

These similarities and differences between the three movements can be illustrated by way of the journalistic compass that was introduced in Chapter 1 (see Figure 5.1), and the compass can also be used to illustrate how the constructive journalism movement itself has developed from its inception in 2008. This development has progressed along both axes: passive–active (the *purpose* of journalism) and representative–deliberative (the *perspective* of journalism). When it comes to the issue of how passive or active constructive journalists should be, the founders were both rather imprecise. This book has described how Gyldensted and Haagerup included examples of active journalism in their early works that fall well outside the parameters of what they today consider to be constructive journalism, and the continuum of active journalism, which has been developed as part of this book (see Chapter 3), delineates how constructive journalism is considerably less active than its predecessors from the nineteenth and twentieth centuries.

Constructive journalism has not only developed along the horizontal axis where the purpose of journalism is delineated. For the interest in including the public and facilitating public debates corresponds with the perspective of journalism, that is delineated as the vertical axis. While it, from the very beginning, was an important part of the public journalism movement to have a deliberative perspective, where private citizens were included in the news

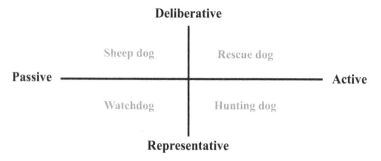

Figure 5.1 The journalistic compass.

media, it might best be described as a later addition to constructive journalism. But it is a development that ties the three movements from the nineteenth, twentieth, and twenty-first centuries even closer together, since servicing the public has become important for all. The active journalists at the turn of the last century were pioneers, when it came to servicing the public, since newspapers until then often functioned as views-papers. Before then the publishers "used the newspaper to propagate" (Ward, 2004, 189) their own ideas, and to service political, religious, commercial, or other organized interests.

That changed, when public service became the ultimate end for journalists and journalism, as Joseph Pulitzer described it at the turn of the last century (1904, 46). The same consideration for the public also prompted the formation of the public journalism movement a century later, since the proponents, supporters, and practitioners believed that the profession had lost contact with the public that journalists and news organizations claimed to work for. All of this is a reminder that journalism is continuously evolving, and that constructive journalism is still developing, and this latter conclusion should come as no surprise for those who has witnessed the birth and followed the upbringing of constructive journalism. By their own admission, the two founders – especially in the movement's infancy – vowed to keep definitions of constructive journalism open, and while the previous chapters have shown that such an open approach has advantages, the two previous movements to do more than present problems are a reminder that there are also disadvantages. Some of the disadvantages are now showing more and more.

Some news organizations and individual news persons – indeed some nations – now claim to be doing constructive journalism, while the principles and practices on which they base their work are clearly at odds with what the founders have intended. In their later works, the founders and several supporters have therefore also found it necessary to address what they have, at times, referred to as "myths" (Gyldensted & Bjerre, 2014) and "booby traps" (Haagerup, 2017, 141–143). The latter refers to the fact that such misunderstandings can be explosive in nature. One of these misunderstandings that the founders have seen a need to correct is that constructive journalism amounts to puff pieces that are excessively complimentary about products, projects, persons, organizations, nations, and other things. This has become important since journalists, editors, and owners of news organizations in some authoritarian regimes have embraced the concept and some supporters of constructive journalism have described this as "hijacking."[6]

This book has described these disadvantages with conceptual unclarity and discussed the importance of conceptual elasticity, when it came to both the rise and the fall of past movements. However, for several reasons, constructive journalism seems to have a better chance of making it in newsrooms – and classrooms, not to forget – in the long run. One of these reasons has do with the fact that both founders from the beginning have pointed to constructive journalism's historical contingencies – even if these contingencies have not been developed much before the publication of this book. The public journalism movement was criticized for not making these connections clear in time and therefore missed an opportunity to tie its work to some of the foundational principles in journalism. The founders of the active movements from the nineteenth and twentieth centuries were also criticized for not clarifying principles and practices, and in each case heated debates and discussions ensued.

Another reason why constructive journalism might have a better chance of standing the test of time has to do with the conservative approach to what active journalism entails. As part of the active journalism around the turn of the last century, journalists, editors, and owners engaged in projects that were meant to solve every conceivable societal problem, and the most ambitious practitioners believed that newspapers had better prerequisites for taking on this responsibility than all other social actors, including the various branches of government. The active journalists of the twentieth century demanded less of themselves, their colleagues, and competitors, when it came to how many problems journalism should solve and how active journalists should engage in the problem-solving. But public journalism was, on the other hand, founded in the belief that it was members of the general public that should be engaged in the problem-solving, and that turned out to be difficult. As one observer noted, public journalism's diagnosis of the ills of traditional journalism is not matched by an understanding of what the public will engage in.[7]

In comparison with the two prior movements, constructive journalism holds journalists less responsible for public welfare – it is "less active," as the previous chapters have shown – and does not envision private citizens as primary problem-solvers. As such, constructive journalism is based on a more restrictive and, in some ways, more realistic model of journalism. Important is also that constructive journalism is based on a less antagonistic model than the two previous movements. Supporters of the active journalism at the turn of the last century criticized other types of journalists and journalism harshly. "The old journalism" was an expression Hearst's newspaper, *The Journalism*, used often; Pulitzer's *The World* denounced the *New York Times* as "derelicts of journalism" (cf. Campbell, 2001); and the defenders of the counteractive approach did not refrain from responding in irreconcilable ways. Debates over the roles and responsibilities of journalism were less heated a hundred years later when the public journalism movement became popular, but even so, there were repeated skirmishes between the two sides.

This is less of a problem with constructive journalism – and for obvious reasons. While not withholding criticism of some of the pressing problems of more traditional types of journalism, the founders of constructive journalism have, from the beginning, acknowledged some of the good things that traditional journalism can contribute with, and Gyldensted, Haagerup, and other supporters of constructive journalism have gone to great lengths to describe how they are also themselves rooted in this same historical tradition. For Haagerup, Gyldensted, and some of the later supporters of constructive journalism, it is not a question of practicing one or the other type of journalism. From the very first public introduction of the concept of constructive news, Haagerup referred to "the tyranny of the or" (2008). His point was – and is - that it should not be just one or another model in journalism, and in a later book, he explains that "(c)onstructive news is not an alternative to critical reporting. It is a supplementary news tool in the editorial toolbox" (2017, 143).

Collaboration between journalistic practitioners and researchers

For these reasons, constructive journalism stands a better chance of becoming a more permanent fixture in newsrooms than its two predecessors, but there are other things to consider if that is to be the case. First and foremost, there is the question of the concept itself. The two founders have left the definition of constructive journalism open from the beginning, and over the years, they have continuously introduced new points and perspectives to be considered. Some of these new points and perspectives have restricted what constructive journalism is. Others points and perspectives have supplemented the existing components of constructive journalism. At the same time, more and more journalistic practitioners around the world have embarked on their own constructive journalism projects and have experimented with ways in which constructive journalism can become part of the everyday practice. All of this have affected how the concept is perceived today, and on the basis of the studies, the best way to define the concept as it stands today might be:

> Constructive journalism call on journalists, editors, and others in the news media to present problems as well as potentials (what works already or what could work in the future) to reflect the world more accurately. For some constructive journalists presenting potentials is an end in itself, for others this is simply the means to another end, namely, to help society solve its problems.

This definition might be subject to change in the coming years, since the authority, when it comes to what constructive journalism is, has been widely delegated, and the experiments still develop.[8] But one of the ways in which we, journalistic practitioners and researchers alike, can give constructive journalism the time it might need to fully develop and become a source of inspiration for future journalists is to be more precise about both what it is and what it can accomplish. Both require a closer cooperation between journalistic practitioners and researchers, and here there is much to be learned from the public journalism movement where this cooperation was built in from the beginning. While Davis Merritt contributed with practical experience from newsrooms, Jay Rosen could offer theoretical insights that he had picked up over the years as a researcher. It was a matter of not keeping "ideas confined to campus," Rosen later explained (1999, 32).

Both of them, journalistic practice and research, are important if we are to become better at defining what constructive journalism is and what constructive journalism amounts to. This book has primarily focused on the first, and when it comes to the latter, studies of the effects of constructive journalism have, to some degree, been part of the movement from the beginning. Gyldensted came to believe in the importance of constructive journalism after having studied how people reacted to news stories with more or less negative framing (2011), and one of the pioneering researchers, Karen McIntyre, also studied the effects from early on. Her dissertation from 2015 is based on a study where she found that when an audience was exposed to journalism with positive angles and suggestions for solutions, respondents expressed stronger intentions to engage in solutions-oriented behavior than people exposed to negative framing (McIntyre, 2015). Since then, more and more researchers have worked together with journalists – or have followed the work of practitioners – in order to study the effects of constructive journalism. This has already resulted in a remarkable number of studies within just a few years.

Some researchers have studied how constructive journalism affects the practice, for example, when it comes to the use of visuals, such as photography (See Lough & McIntyre, 2019), while others have studied who the constructive practitioners are and how these journalists and editors have responded to constructive journalism (see, e.g., Krüger et al. 2022). Still others have studied the effects of constructive journalism when it comes to news sources and news audiences (see, e.g., Hermans & Prins, 2020; Overgaard, 2021; Swijtink et al., 2022; Thier et al., 2019; van Antwerpen et al., 2022). Several important studies have been presented already and more are on their way, but most if not all of these studies are based on small sampling sizes; on specific national, regional, or local contexts; on select issues; and on particular news formats and platforms. What is needed in the coming years is also empirical studies with more reach and comparative relevance, so that we can get a better understanding of the effects on constructive journalism on both news reporters, news sources, and news audiences, more broadly.

To understand how readers, listeners, and viewers respond to and are affected by constructive journalism is of particular relevance. For if constructive journalists are to envy the first generation of active journalists, editors, and owners of newspapers, it should first and foremost be for their success, when it came to engaging their audience. While the practitioners of the movement around the turn of the last century have been rightly criticized for many things, this generation demonstrated on an almost daily basis that if your journalism can inspire people and engage them to take part in public life, private citizens are also more inclined to become part of a news audience. This reciprocal relation created a powerful dynamic 150 years ago, and today, where journalism and the news media are confronted with many challenges – not least commercially and financially – studying the effects of constructive journalism is surely one of the most pertinent for journalistic practitioners and researchers alike.

Notes

1 Pulitzer Hall at Columbia University's Graduate School of Journalism is an example of this.
2 Journalism scholars have used different concepts to describe this approach to journalism. The media historian W. Joseph Campbell, for example, uses the concept of a "counter-activist" paradigm to describe this development (2006, 6).
3 As noted in the previous chapter (particularly Chapter 2), there have been other minor movements in the history of journalism. Here, it might be useful to distinguish between movements with a more generic approach, such as constructive journalism and active journalism, and the more narrowly focused movements, such as peace journalism, which is preoccupied with a particular idea or issue.
4 Jay Rosen collected these and other critical statements about public journalism (1999, 25).
5 A couple of other researchers have noted the top-down and bottom-up approaches. W. Joseph Campbell refers to a "bottom-up" process, when it comes to public journalism (2001, 183), while Unni From and Nete Nørgaard Kristensen have noted that constructive journalism "emerged bottom-up from newsroom practitioners" (2018, 715).
6 The fear of constructive journalism being equated with "puff pieces" and also being "hijacked" by news persons, news organizations, and even other nations has been addressed at several conferences and seminars about constructive journalism. One such example was when the Constructive Institute at Aarhus University and Centre for Journalism at the University of Southern co-hosted a conference in 2022 about the state of affairs in the field.
7 "What Public Journalism Knows about Journalism but Doesn't Know about 'Public'" was a telling title used by Michael Schudson to express this point (1999, 118). Other scholars, such as John Durham Peters (1999), have concluded the same, and it has been suggested that the most successful public journalism experiments in cities such as Spokane, Madison, Akron, and Wichita probably owe something to those cities' long histories of labor or populist activism (Friedland cf. Pauly, 1999, 145).
8 There are good opportunities to stay up to date about the developments of constructive journalism, solutions journalism, and other associated approaches to journalism. The Constructive Institute at Aarhus University in Denmark regularly updates its website with news about conferences, seminars, master classes, new publications, project by fellows, and so forth (www.constructiveinstitute.org). The Solutions Journalism Network shares many resources on the website, including material for reporters and newsroom, lecturers and students, and mission-driving organizations. This is also the digital home for the Solutions Story Tracker, which is a curated database with responses to social problems and inspirational journalistic work within this field (www.solutionsjournalism.org). Finally, there are individuals who do an impressive job, when it comes to keeping track of developments. One of these is Kyser Lough who has contributed with important studies within this

field over the years, and he keeps track of an array of publications relating to both constructive journalism and solutions journalism. The publications on Lough's lists include books, chapters, doctoral dissertations, and thesis – also in other languages that English American (www.kyserlough.com/solutionsjournalism.html).

References

Bro, Peter (2004) *Aktionsjournalistik* [*Action Journalism*]. Odense: Syddansk Universitetsforlag.

Bro, Peter and Cathrine Gyldensted (2021) "Constructive journalism: Portraying the world accurately through positive psychology." In *Reporting Beyond the Problem: From Civic Journalism to Solutions Journalism*, edited by Karen McIntyre and Nicole Dahmen, 29–46, New York: Peter Lang.

Campbell, W. Joseph (2001) *Yellow Journalism: Puncturing the Myths, Defining the Legacies*. London: Praeger.

Campbell, W. Joseph (2006) *The Year That Defined American Journalism: 1897 and the Clash of Paradigms*. New York: Routledge.

Frankel, Max (1995) "Fix-It journalism." *New York Times Magazine*, May 21.

From, Unni and Nete Nørgaard Kristensen (2018) "Rethinking constructive journalism by means of service journalism." Journalism Practice 12 (6): 714–729.

Gyldensted, Cathrine (2020) *Blev du Klogere: Sådan Forbedrer du den Offentlige Samtale* [Did You Get Smarter: How to Improve Public Conversation]. København: Forlaget Højskolerne.

Gyldensted, Cathrine and Malene Bjerre (2014) *Håndbog i Konstruktiv Journalistic* [Handbook in Constructive Journalism]. Århus: Ajour.Haagerup, Ulrik (2008) "Konstruktive nyheder" [Constructive News]. *Politiken*, December 6.

Haagerup, Ulrik (2017) *Constructive News: How to Save the Media and Democracy with Journalism of Tomorrow*. Aarhus, Denmark: Aarhus University Press.

Haas, Tanni (2007) *The Pursuit of Public Journalism: Theory, Practice, and Criticism*. New York: Routledge.

Hermans, Liesbeth and Tineke Prins (2020) "Interest matters: The effects of constructive news reporting on Millennials' emotions and engagement." *Journalism* 23 (5): 1064–1081.

Krüger, Uwe, Markus Beiler, Thilko Gläßgen, Michael Kees and Maximilian Küstermann (2022) "Neutral observers or advocates for societal transformation? Role Orientation of constructive journalists in Germany." *Media and Communication* 10 (3): 64–77.

Lough, Kyser and Karen McIntyre (2019) "Visualizing the solution: An analysis of the images that accompany solutions-oriented news stories." *Journalism* 20 (4): 583–599.

McIntyre, Karen (2015) *Constructive Journalism: The Effects of Positive Emotions and Solution Information in News Stories*. Doctoral Dissertation, University of North Carolina, Chapel Hill, NC.

Merritt, Davis (1995) *Public Journalism and Public Life*. Mahwah, NJ: Lawrence Erlbaum Associates.

Overgaard, Christian Staal Bruun (2021) "Mitigating the consequences of negative news: How constructive journalism enhances self-efficacy and news credibility." *Journalism*. Advance Online Publication First.

Pauly, J. John (1999) "Journalism and the Sociology of Public Life." In *The Idea of Public Journalism*, edited by Theodore Glasser, 152–172. New York: Guildford Press.

Peters, John Durham (1999) "Public journalism and democratic theory." In *The Idea of Public Journalism*, edited by Theodore Glasser, 99–117, New York: Guildford Press.

Pulitzer, Joseph (1904) *The School of Journalism at Columbia University*. New York: Columbia University Press.

Rosen, Jay (1999) "The action of the idea." In *The Idea of Public Journalism*, edited by Theodore L. Glasser, 21–48, New York: Guilford Press.

Schudson, Michael (1999) "What public journalism knows about journalism but doesn't know about 'public'." In *The Idea of Public Journalism*, edited by Theodore Glasser, 118–133, New York: Guildford Press.

Swijtink, N., Prins, T., Hermans, L. and Hietbrink, N. (2022) "An informed audience: The effects of constructive television news on emotions and knowledge." *Journalism*. Onlinefirst publication.

Thier, Kathryn, Jesse Abdenour, Brent Walth and Nicole Smith Dahmen (2019) "A narrative solution: The relationship between solutions journalism, narrative transportation, and news trust. *Journalism* 22 (10): 2511–2530.

van Antwerpen, N., Searston, R. A., Turnbull, D., Hermans, L. and Kovacevic, P. (2022) "The effects of constructive journalism techniques on mood, comprehension, and trust." *Journalism*. Onlinefirst publication.

Ward, Stephen J. A. (2004) *The Invention of Journalism Ethics: The Path to Objectivity and Beyond*. Montreal: McGill-Queen's University Press.

Index

Note: *Italic* page numbers refer to figures and page numbers followed by "n" denote endnotes.

action journalism 12, 18, 19, 22, 75, 81, 82
active journalism 20–23, 25, 31, 42, 59n7, 69, 72, 83, 86; approaches to 42–50; degrees of 50–55, *52*; objectivity in 55–58; rise and fall of 33–37
active journalism continuum 51, *52*
active journalists 7, 9, 12, 33, 42, 51, 54, 57, 71, 73, 75, 76, 85, 86, 88
actors 74–76
advocacy continuum 59n5
advocacy journalism 52
Akron Beacon Journal 25, 47–48

Bjerre, Malene 54, 59n8, 72, 74; *Textbook in Constructive Journalism* 56–57
Bly, Nellie 20, 38n3
booby traps 33, 85
Bornstein, David 5
bottom-up process 83, 89n5
Broder, David 24

Campbell, Cole C. 25, 48, 79n7
Campbell, W. Joseph 13n1, 28, 51, 54, 58n3, 59n6, 83, 89n2, 89n5
Carey, James 5, 6, 34
Cavling, Henrik 22, 23, 36, 81–83; *From America* 22
Cavling Prize 82
Center for Civic Journalism 27, 31
Chalaby, Jean 38n4
Charity, Arthur 26
The Charlotte Observer 25–26, 48

Cisneros affair 49, 53, 58n3
Cisneros, Evangeline 19
civic journalism 38n6, 63, 82
community journalism 18, 24, 38n6, 63, 82
conceptual elasticity 11
conceptual elusiveness 35, 37
conservative reform movement 52, 53
Constructive Institute 4, 10, 14n10, 14n12, 30, 32, 47, 58n2, 65, 77, 78n1, 78n2, 89n6, 89n8
Constructive Journalism (Haagerup) 46, 47
"Constructive Journalism: Applying Positive Psychology Techniques to News Production" 34
Constructive Journalism: From Idea to Story (Jørgensen and Risbro) 58n2, 69
constructive news 3, 13n3, 29, 44, 64, 65
Constructive News 29–31, 35
A Constructive News Story: Showdown with the Press's Negative World View (Haagerup) 3, 11, 29
contemporary news media 73; negativity bias of 29
continuums 51, *52*, *52*, 59n5

Danish Broadcasting Company 3, 4, 14n11, 32, 45, 64, 70
"definitional elusiveness" 35
Dewey, John 25, 38n5
Did You Get Smarter: How to Improve Public Conversation (Gyldensted) 32–33, 77

"East River murder mystery" 53
Editor and Publisher 27
editors 1, 2, 4, 7, 9, 12, 17–21, 23, 24, 27, 31, 34, 42, 43, 46, 48–51, 54–57, 62–64, 66–67, 71–76, 81–83, 85, 86, 88
elasticity 35, 37
The Elements of Journalism (Rosenstiel and Kovach) 7

Fishers, Caroline 59n5
From America (Cavling) 22
From Mirrors to Movers (Gyldensted) 4, 11, 28, 35, 43, 46, 47, 67, 72, 76, 79n6
From, Unni 71, 89n5
Fyens Stiftstidende 47, 48, 58n2

Galtung, Johan 23–24, 65; "The Structure of Foreign News" 23
gearshifts 17
The Guardian 47, 72, 79n6
Gyldensted, Cathrine 3–4, 9–12, 29, 30, 33, 35, 45, 46, 48, 50, 54, 56, 59n8, 64–66, 71, 74–77, 78n1, 84, 86, 87; *Did You Get Smarter: How to Improve Public Conversation* 32–33, 77; *From Mirrors to Movers* 4, 11, 28, 35, 43, 46, 47, 67, 72, 76, 79n6; *Textbook in Constructive Journalism* 56–57

Haagerup, Ulrik 3, 9–11, 13n3, 28–32, 35, 44–48, 55–57, 63–65, 67, 70, 71, 75–77, 78n1, 84, 86, 87; *Constructive Journalism* 46, 47; *A Constructive News Story: Showdown with the Press's Negative World View* 3, 11, 29
Haas, Tanni 27, 59n11
Habermas, Jürgen 25, 38n5
Hallin, Daniel 69, 70, 72, 78n5
Hanitzsch, Thomas 59n5
Harmsworth, Alfred 1, 21, 36
Hearst, William Randolph 1, 2, 12, 18–23, 36, 37n2, 44, 49–51, 54, 58n3, 58n4, 59n7, 67, 81, 83, 86

The Idea of Journalism 35
impartiality 51, 53–57, 59n7
The Invention of Journalism Ethics: The Path to Objectivity and Beyond (Ward) 55–56, 59n9

Jørgensen, Kristina Lund 78n1; *Constructive Journalism: From Idea to Story* 69
The Journal 18, 19, 22, 23, 36, 49–50, 53, 58n3, 59n4, 59n6, 67, 68
journalism 1; active types of 34, *34*; history of 17, 32–34, 37n1, 50, 58, 75, 89n3; immediate future of 82; models of 23; similarities and differences between active types of 83–87, *84*; social responsibility of 82; sourcing practices in 73, *73*; types of 37n2
The Journalism 86
"journalism as government." 21, 81
"Journalism as Government" (Stead) 21
"journalism as information" 37n2
"journalism of entertainment" 37n2
journalism researchers 1–3, 24
journalism scholars 89n2
journalism schools 4, 6, 8, 13n7, 23, 29, 32, 41–43, 62, 65, 77, 81, 82
journalism that does things 19, 21, 50, 51, 62, 75, 81, 83
Journalisten 13n4
journalistic compass 7–9, *8,* 14n9, 84, *84*
journalistic ideologies 17
journalistic practices 9–13, 62–63; approaches to constructive journalism 63–68, *66*; what is relevant for journalism 68–72; who is relevant for journalism 72–76
journalistic practitioners 1, 6, 38n6, 44, 68; collaboration between researchers and 87–89
journalistic precedents 9–13, 17–18; constructive journalism of twenty-first century 28–33; new journalism of nineteenth century 18–23; public journalism of twentieth century 23–27; rise and fall of active journalism 33–37
journalistic principles 9–13, 41–42; approaches to objectivity in active journalism 55–58; degrees of active journalism 50–55, *52*; journalists partake in solutions 48–50; journalists should present potentials 44–46; journalists should present problems 43–44; journalists should promote solutions 46–48

journalists: new generation of 62; partake in solutions 48–50; present and future generations of 63; should present potentials 44–46; should present problems 43–44; should promote solutions 46–48
The Journalist's Creed 6

Kovach, Bill: *The Elements of Journalism* 7

"the Lene effect" 64, 66, 67, 70, 74
lifestyle journalism 71
Lippmann, Walter: *Public Opinion* 74
The London Evening Standard 21
Los Angeles Times 49
Lough, Kyser 14n8, 89–90n8

markers 74–76
May, Gerd Maria 65, 78n1, 78n2
McIntyre, Karen 10, 14n8, 32, 33, 45, 88
media history, cyclic movements in 17
Merritt, Davis 24–25, 28, 35, 49, 53, 57, 58, 67, 83, 88; *Public Journalism and Public Life* 26; *Public Journalism: Theory and Practice* 25
modern journalism 23
Muckraking: The Journalism That Changed America (Serrin and Serrin) 20
myths 11, 36, 54, 59n8, 85

negative journalism 29
negativity bias 30; of contemporary news media 29
neutrality 12, 42, 49, 51, 53, 55, 57
new journalism 37n1, 81; of nineteenth century 18–23
Newness, George 21
news media 71, 73, 75, 81, 89; publication in 65
news organizations 3–7, 9, 12, 17–19, 26, 27, 34, 42–44, 46, 48, 50, 51, 56, 57, 63, 66, 68, 71, 72, 75, 78n1, 82, 85
newspapers 18, 19, 22, 83, 85, 86; Danish 48, 77; Gannett newspaper chain 27; neutral 5; new generation of 2; in New York City and St. Louis 23; policy on standards and ethics 54; side, editors and owners of 2, 86

newsrooms 1–3, 6, 8, 18, 21–25, 27, 34, 35, 42, 46, 51, 58, 62–65, 70–72, 77, 82, 85, 87, 88
news stories 5, 8, 9, 17, 29, 30, 44, 45, 51, 56, 57, 63–66, 71–73, 75, 83, 88
The New York Journal 18
The New York Press 59n7
The New York Times 18, 53, 59n6, 76
The New York Tribune 50
The New York World 20
Nørgaard Kristensen, Nete 71, 89n5
Northcliffe, Lord 1, 2, 12, 21, 23, 81, 83

objectivity 54; in active journalism 55–58, 59n9, 59n10
Ochs, Adolph 18
Ochs, Alfred 53, 59n7
old journalism 18, 44, 49, 86
owners 1, 2, 4, 6, 7, 9, 12, 17–19, 27, 34, 42, 43, 46, 48, 50, 51, 56, 57, 62, 66, 68, 71, 72, 74, 75, 81–83, 85, 86, 88

The Pall Mall Gazette 21
passive journalism 54, 69
Patterson, Thomas 43
peace journalism 24, 33
"The People Project: Solving It Ourselves" 25
PERMA-model 78n1
Peters, John Durham 89n7
pillars 77–78; of solutions journalism 79n8
political journalism 62, 70
positive journalism 32, 45, 66
positive psychology 4, 10, 30, 45, 66, 78n1
potential–problem approach 66, 66–68
potentials, defined as 31
The Practice of Journalism (Williams and Martin) 65
Prize, Cavling 43
"proactive neutrality" 49, 53
problem-based journalism 30, 63
problem-focused journalism 44, 82
problem-holders 73, 76
problem-solvers 73, 76
problem-solving journalism 14n11, 86
problem-solving reporting 14n11
public journalism 28, 31–32, 35, 36, 38n5, 38n6, 49, 57, 71, 73, 82; as conservative reform movement 52; as "Fix-It

96 Index

Journalism" 53; mechanics of 63; practitioners of 83; promoters and practitioners of 54; of twentieth century 23–27
Public Journalism and Public Life (Merritt) 26
public journalism movement 5, 44, 47, 48, 50, 52, 59n11, 63, 79n9, 83, 84, 86, 88
Public Journalism: Theory and Practice (Rosen and Merritt) 25
public journalists 24, 28, 50, 57, 75
Public Opinion (Lippmann) 74
public service 5–9, *8,* 13n7, 22, 23, 85
"Public Service the Ultimate End" 41
public welfare 20, 81, 86
Pulitzer, Joseph 1, 2, 5–6, 12, 19–24, 28, 36, 37n2, 41, 42, 44, 49, 50, 54, 58n4, 59n7, 62, 73, 81, 82, 85, 86
Pulitzer Prize 6, 23, 25, 74, 82

Remington, Frederick 58n3
Reporters d'Espoirs 5, 13n6
Riis, Jacob A. 28, 43, 78n3
Risbro, Jakob 78n1; *Constructive Journalism: From Idea to Story* 69
Roosevelt, Theodore 29
Rosenberg, Tina 5, 76
Rosen, Jay 24–25, 27, 28, 31, 35, 38n5, 49, 50, 53, 57, 71, 73, 83, 88, 89n4; *Public Journalism: Theory and Practice* 25
Rosenstiel, Tom: *The Elements of Journalism* 7
Rosling, Hans 30
Ruge, Maria 65
Ruge, Marie 23
Rusbridger, Alan 79n6

Schudson, Michael 9, 13n2, 28, 37n2, 52, 89n7
Serrin, Judith: *Muckraking: The Journalism That Changed America* 20
Serrin, William: *Muckraking: The Journalism That Changed America* 20
service journalism 71
social responsibility 52, 82
solution-focused journalism 82
Solution Journalism Network 5, 68, 77, 79n8, 89n8

solutions journalism 5, 14n8, 68; pillars of 79n8
Solutions Story Tracker 89n8
"somewhat vague" concept 10
sphere of consensus 69, *70*
sphere of deviance 69, *70*
sphere of legitimate controversy 69, *70*
Statue of Liberty 20
Stead, William T. 21, 23, 81, 83; "Journalism as Government" 21
STEP-model 78n1, 78n2
stereotypes 73, 74; typology of 75
St. Louis Post-Dispatch 25, 48, 79n7
"The Structure of Foreign News" (Galtung) 23
Swedish Broadcasting Corporation 72, 73

"Taking Back Our Neighborhoods" 25–26
Textbook in Constructive Journalism (Gyldensted and Bjerre) 56–57
Thompson, Hunter S. 18
Thörnqvist, Ingrid 72, 73
The Times 53, 54, 59n7
traditional journalism 27, 31, 45, 68–69, 71, 86
traditional problem-oriented journalism 68–69, 74
translators 74, 75
twenty-first century, constructive journalism of 28–33

Verne, Jules 20
Vietnam war, journalism coverage of 69

Ward, Stephen: *The Invention of Journalism Ethics: The Path to Objectivity and Beyond* 55–56, 59n9
The Washington Post 24, 54
The Wichita Eagle 24
Wiener, Joel 13n1
Williams, Walter 6, 13n7; *The Practice of Journalism* 65
Wolfe, Tom 18
The World 20, 22, 36, 50, 51, 54, 58n3, 59n4, 59n6, 68, 73, 74, 86

yellow journalism 36, 54
yellow press 59n7

Zelizer, Barbie 36, 63, 79n9